fragments

Wilma Daugherty

Wilma Daugherty

fragments:

Stories of Another Time

Drinian Press/
Huron, Ohio

fragments: Stories of Another Time

Drinian Press
P.O. Box 63
Huron, Ohio 44839

www.DrinianPress.com.
Biography, Memoir

Cover design © 2007 Drinian Press.
Cover photo by Nancy Brady Smith

Library of Congress Control Number: 2007927497

ISBN-10: 0-9785165-4-0
ISBN-13: 978-0-9785165-4-3

DrinianPress.com
Printed in the United States

To Michael and Marty,
the grandchildren,
and

in loving memory of Bill

ACKNOWLEDGEMENTS

fragments: Stories of Another Time
is a collection of short stories and memoirs by Wilma
Daugherty. In addition to newly published stories, it
includes selected readings from two previously published
books. *There Was a Time* was first released in 1996 and
Along the Way followed in 1998. Both were published
through "Friends of the Firelands Writing Center" in
Huron, Ohio. Drinian Press wishes to acknowledge the
Friends of the Firelands and thank them for their
cooperation and assistance with this new collection. In
particular, Dr. Larry Smith provided archival support for
the project and has encouraged this effort to preserve an
important piece of our Midwestern literary heritage.
Nancy Brady Smith deserves special recognition for her
hours of work transcribing manuscripts and proofing the
final text.

R.B. Smith
Drinian Press
May 2007

Book I

From: *There Was a Time*

Childhood

Wife and Mother Days

Later Years

Book II

From: *Along the Way*

Getting Educated

Dance of Youth

Some Things Only Happen Once

Book III

Time Passes, Memories Linger

Book I

There Was a Time

Stuff Gramma Taught Me

Gramma taught me how to skip! I couldn't get the hang of it. She showed me how to hop on one foot and then the other and go faster and faster and there you are skipping. We must have been a funny looking pair as we hopped unsteadily on our way to school.

Gramma taught school where I attended the first grade. We walked together each morning. We usually sang *Off We Go into the Wild Blue Yonder* or *It's a Grand Old Flag.* If it got late we sang a little faster. If we came to a walk with a hopscotch, we both jumped through it without a hitch and without missing a note. Sometimes we went by way of the field where there was a path which we called (and rightly) Dog Do Alley. If Gramma told me we had to hurry I told her I'd make my legs go in and out faster. Gramma always laughed.

One day I asked her, "What does feisty mean?"

"Feisty, who told you about feisty?"

"Dad said you were feisty." Gramma chuckled. "Feisty, why that means I'm a good gramma."

"Will I be feisty, Gramma?"

"I hope so."

Gramma taught me all kinds of neat things, like how to crack my gum. It's hard to explain about making the gum all flat inside your mouth, then sticking it against your teeth and somehow drawing in your breath. Over and over I tried and nothing happened, and then suddenly a wonderful pop.

"What's all that racket?" Father asked from the front seat.

Gramma just laughed. "A kid's not worth his salt if he can't pop his gum."

3

fragments

In our backyard she taught me how to make wonderful sounds by blowing through a blade of grass. A thin narrow blade made a weird screech like a cat caterwauling she called it. A thicker blade made a lonely sound like a train going far, far away. That's the sound I liked best, although it could make you happy and sad all at once. A thick blade made a blubbery sound that Gramma said wasn't quite polite.

When we traveled with Gramma, we counted cows. My sister always won. I guess there were more cows on her side or maybe she counted faster. Or maybe I had more cemeteries on my side where I had to bury my cows. One long trip I was way ahead for the first time. We were almost home and we came to this big cemetery. There go all my cows! Gramma looked at me but didn't say a word. A road divided the cemetery in the middle. Gramma turned in and there went all my cows and my sister's cows, too.
"Oops! Wrong turn!" was all Gramma said.

"Could we fly, Gramma?"
"In a plane, you mean?"
"No, like a bird, if we flapped our arms and got a good start."
"We'll never know till we try, will we? We'll climb on top of the chicken coop and look over the situation," Gramma said.
It looked pretty high. "Just in case," Gramma said, "we'll pile straw on the ground for a safe landing."
We stood up there on top of the chicken coop and flapped our arms just for practice. Chickens squawked and our old dog barked furiously. Then we took off. Next thing I knew, we were all tangled up in the straw.
"We flew, didn't we Gramma?"
"We sure did!" Gramma said, and she laughed.

4

fragments

"Are there really elves, Gramma?"

"I never really saw one," Gramma said, "but that doesn't prove there aren't any, now does it?"

"Well if there are elves, where would we find them?"

"In the woods, under a bush very early in the morning."

"Tomorrow?"

We walked hand in hand, very early, the dew still on the ground. "Do you see anything?" Gramma whispered. "Be very quiet, just barely breathe."

"I saw a flash of blue under that bush. Do you think that was an elf, Gramma?"

"It could have been. That's probably nearer than anyone has ever come to seeing one."

"We're lucky, aren't we Gramma?"

If you lie down in a meadow, away from houses and people, and put your ear flat to the ground and close your eyes and be very, very still you can hear a soft whirring sound. Gramma said it was the world going around. We kept that secret, a wonderfully exciting thing to do, like you knew something no one else knew.

"Will you be in a wheelchair, Gramma?"

"Maybe."

"I'll push you, Gramma."

We were sitting on the sea wall discussing great truths. The sky was like crushed strawberries and soft gray. The lake was rippling silver.

"Will you die someday, Gramma?"

"Of course, everyone dies."

"What happens when you die?"

"My body won't be any good by that time. It'll be all worn out like old clothes. The real me is here inside. I'll leave that old part and go off where I'm going. You'll sing, won't you, Love?"

"I'll sing, Gramma. I'll sing, *Off We Go Into the Wild Blue*

Yonder. "

"Did you know that little bits of dust make a beautiful sunset?"

"Like now?"

"Like now," she said. "After I'm gone whenever you see a beautiful sunset you'll think, 'there's Gramma!'"

She held my hand and we laughed.

I don't know what kids do without their grammas!

Swimming

It was so hot you could push it away with both hands. All I could think of was cool clean sparkling water. If only I could persuade Dad to take us to Chain's Schoolhouse to swim!

Chain's Schoolhouse was a one-room school where my mother had once taught all eight grades. It was no longer used except for special events in the country. The building was in a clearing among tall oak trees. Behind it the creek had been dammed up and stones piled up so that the more daring kids could step out and grab a strong vine, swing out over the water, and drop with a splash into a deep pool of clear rushing water. It was a heavenly place to picnic and swim.

It was Wednesday. Dad closed the store at noon. All he really wanted to do when he got home was to sit on the porch with his shoes off and complain through the screen door to Mother about how hot it was in the store and how lucky she was to be home all day.

Mother wiped the sweat off her face with her old blue apron, kept right on stirring the spaghetti sauce on the hot stove with one hand, and grabbed my little sister off the floor with the other. She answered the phone, called my little brother, and smiled lovingly at my father, nodding her head in agreement. At the refrigerator she got him a tall glass of lemonade.

This looked like a good time to approach Dad about the swimming.

"Dad, how about taking us to Chain's Schoolhouse for a swim?"

"Who's us?"

"You know, the kids in the neighborhood. It's so hot!"

"Uhh, " my father said.

"You could swim with us. You're such a good swimmer; I never knew anyone could swim better'n you."

"Uhh," my father said.

"I love swinging on that old vine and dropping into that cool water. Remember when you showed me how to do that? Remember how scared I was? Huh, Dad?"

"Yes I remember. You were just a little tyke." He smiled.

I held my breath and waited.

"Well, all right, " he said. "Round up the kids. Not too many now."

Next door. "Hey, Wertzy, we're going swimming."

Across the street. "Listen up, Cece, Dad's taking us swimming!"

A block away for John and Eddie.

At Ralphy's house no one ever yelled. You knocked on the door and asked Mrs. Ross politely if Ralphy could go.

"Who's going, who's driving? How long will you be gone?" she asked.

After careful consideration she gave her consent and we were off to get the other kids.

Dad drove the big Studebaker up to the front door. "Hop in kids; the sooner we get there, the sooner we'll be cooled off."

We pulled up the two little seats from the floor. That made room for nine not counting my father. That is, if I put a board between the two little seats. That's where I always sat. The boys said it was a girl's place. It was hard and uncomfortable, but today I didn't care. I was going swimming! I didn't even get mad when the boys pushed the board off and I fell to the floor. They giggled and said it was an accident. I just laughed and thought of that first plunge into cold water.

fragments

The Studebaker was stifling. The hot air blowing in over nine sticky kids was even worse. All I could think of was that first cool dip. I'd just lie on my back and look up at the sky and feel like I was in heaven.

"Chain's Schoolhouse!" someone shouted. Dad pulled in to a grassy spot. No one was here. What luck! The boys were out of the car in a flash running and screaming towards the creek. I was last out since my board had fallen off the seat again.

Dad followed the boys. He turned and came slowly back to the car.

"Sorry, honey, you can't go in."

"But why? Why, Dad?"

"I'm afraid the boys, the boys are skinny dipping. "

Too Old for Teeth

When I was a child I liked to sit beside my great-grandmother and listen to her stories of long ago.

She wore voluminous skirts with many pockets in which she carried little things to nibble on. She'd share raisins or dried apricots. She wore a black waist and around her neck a clean white handkerchief pinned in front with a hand-painted brooch.

She had no teeth at all when I knew her. She told me she had lived on a farm five miles from Salineville, Ohio. There were no roads, only railroad tracks led into town.

One morning she got up with a terrible toothache. She couldn't eat or talk or most importantly, get on with her work. As the pain got even more excruciating she decided to go into town to the dentist. She walked all five miles by herself. The dentist pulled every one of her teeth! She walked right back home holding towels over her bleeding mouth. The dentist told her she was too old to get false teeth. She was fifty years old then. She died at the age of one hundred.

The Roller Coaster

Can you imagine anything more exciting than owning your very own roller coaster? My brother, Milt always with impossibly outrageous ideas, decided to build a roller coaster in our backyard. He enlisted the kids in the neighborhood with the promise of free rides as payment.

Our father owned a hardware store and lumber company, so we had access to scraps of lumber which we hauled in a small red wagon. Some of the men who drove trucks for my father were willing, on an off day, to deliver wood to us, and sometimes they would bring a nice long piece that could be used for runners.

The coaster was to be sixty feet long with one dip in the middle. We had to start rather high to get enough momentum to get to the top of the first dip. This presented a problem which we solved by using the chicken coop as a starting place. We found an old trellis which could be used as a ladder. The car was an old wagon with the tongue removed and handles nailed to each side for passengers to hold on to. We painted the wagon bright red and in black letters, named it "Milt's Menace."

The runners were the most difficult. The grooves on each side had to be about two inches deep to take care of the wagon wheels.
Hundreds of pieces were nailed together to make that long stretch of track.

We helped ourselves to nails at my father's store. The nails were kept in huge barrels and weighed out for each customer. I don't know if ours were ever missed. We were careful to help ourselves when my father happened to be out of the store. The clerks just smiled and turned their backs.

The whole project took most of the summer. Each night, dirty and tired, we went to bed eagerly awaiting time to get up and start again.

I made sandwiches for everyone and mothers sent lunches along in paper bags, glad to be rid of their kids for the summer.

My best friend Millie and I were the only girls allowed in on the project, probably because we ran all the errands, did the painting, and lettered "Milt's Menace" on the car.

Finally the great day came when we could try it out. Milt got the first ride as befitted the producer, son of the lumber dealer, and also it happened to be on our lot. We weren't sure that the first steep slope would be enough to get the car over the dip. After that, it was all downhill.

At the end of the ride, the boys dug a wide ditch and one of the men from the store filled it with sand. So when the passenger got to the end, the car simply hit sand and came to a full stop. We thought of everything.

Milt went up the trellis got on the car; Cece gave him a push and he was off! He kept right on track up to the top of the dip with ease and went flying by to the end of the track and into the sand. A great cheer went up! The roller coaster was a success. We toasted each other with root beer.

Now it was time to go public. Millie and I painted a sign and nailed it to the chicken coop. FOR THE THRILL OF YOUR LIFE, RIDE MILT'S MENACE. 5¢ for children, 10¢ for adults. We knew adults wouldn't ride and even if they wanted to, they couldn't possibly fit in the wagon. But we thought it sounded professional.

Then we waited for our first customer. Tony lived right down the street. He came clutching five sticky pennies. I put the pennies in an old soup can which we used in lieu of a cash register. If things went as well as we expected, we could get a large coffee can or even some day a cash register.

We all watched anxiously as Tony bravely sat on the wagon. Down he went, up over the dip and down into the sand pit screaming wildly all the way as you are supposed to do on roller coasters. He was all smiles when he came back.

Day after day kids came from all over town and lined up to ride our coaster. We were getting rich. We had thoughts of building a Ferris wheel next summer. We exchanged our soup can for a five-pound coffee can and had another one in reserve. Adults came in the evening and laughed at the kids as they screamed and jostled to get in place.

Then came the day of disaster. Johnny McCloskey had heard of our coaster. Why he wanted to ride, no one will ever know. Johnny was the kind of boy who was afraid of his own shadow. On Halloween his mother pulled all the shades down and never answered the door. If Johnny saw a masked face, he became hysterical and had to be put to bed. He never was allowed to get dirty or eat anything the other kids ate. But somehow he had persuaded his mother to let him ride. While his parents watched, he gingerly climbed up the trellis and got on the car. He held desperately with both hands and Milt gave him a gentle push. And wouldn't you know it! The car jumped the track and Johnny fell off at the top of the dip. Well, all hell broke loose! His mother grabbed him and screamed and made such a scene, we were all sure he'd broken his neck. Actually, he had a few scratches. We all crowded around while he kicked and screamed and his mother called him, "Poor Baby!" She took him home and called the family doctor.

Next day, she went to my father's store and demanded that the roller coaster be torn down. She made such a fuss that she scared other kids off. Mothers began to forbid their kids to ride. We changed our sign to 3¢ a ride, then 1¢. Inside of a week we were paying kids to ride. As we saw our money dwindling we knew we had lost the battle.

From that time on, Johnny McCloskey was known as

fragments

Poor Baby. And whenever a kid put up a great fuss over nothing we said he was pulling a McCloskey.

Years later when someone would say, "Remember the summer you kids built the roller coaster?" Just for an instant, I'd be filled with the sense of wild excitement and anticipation of that long ago summer.

14

fragments

Christmas

Blue lights on a Christmas tree, softly falling snow outside my window, the silence of remembered bells and peace. That's what Christmas meant to me when I was a child.

There were seven of us children and we started planning weeks in advance for the great day. We earned our own money doing small chores for my parents and grandparents. We spent ten cents on each person, and all that was left over we divided equally between my father and mother. Sometimes, if we had worked hard and avoided the candy store, there might be fifty cents left over for each one. You could buy almost anything in the world for fifty cents!

My little sister Ginny scoffed at ten cent presents. She spent the whole magnificent sum on one wonderful gift. She didn't take turns, but just picked someone out at random as the mood struck her. One year she picked me and I still have the globe of the world she gave me. Sometimes yet I play the old game of shutting my eyes, giving it a whirl, placing my finger on it and that's where I'm going. But I lacked my little sister's courage and could never quite decide to leave anyone out.

We bought each present carefully. Finally, we had been to town dozens of times, had driven the clerks crazy, had bought our gifts wrapped them and stored them away. We said for the hundredth time, "No one is allowed to look in my room for anything!" Signs were posted here and there which stated, in no polite terms, "Stay out, this means you!"

The day before Christmas, we trimmed the tree. The white and shining angel, more beautiful than any new one, was placed on the topmost branch. The bright balls, the silver bird with the lopsided tail, the pictures of Santa Claus we had made in first grade, the pale blue angels we had made in Sunday School all had been exclaimed over as if they were new.

And while we trimmed the tree, all kinds of good things were being prepared in the kitchen. We made numerous trips to test everything. We talked about the gifts we were going to receive. The neighbors must have envied the presents we anticipated. We talked about going to Grandma's, just a block down the street, for Christmas dinner. I think as a family, on the day before Christmas, in that room, we were at our very best. Everyone was important to everyone else. Our happiness was unequaled.

Now, finally, it is bedtime and with great ceremony we hang up our stockings. Three long black ones for the boys, three long white ones for the girls, and a small blue one for the baby.

After everyone is ready for bed, it is time to bring down the presents and place them under the tree. Each child brings his down alone. You stand inside your door, your heart thumping madly. You open it a crack and listen. Someone else is making a trip down to the tree. So you close your door and wait. You open it again. The coast is clear and you start down.

I always liked to be the last. All lights are out except the ones on the tree. The room is long and beautiful. You lay your bundles carefully around so that they won't be given all at once when they are handed out in the morning. As you place yours, you see an odd looking package! Suppose it's for you! You could turn it over and see. But it might be, and that would spoil everything. You shiver at the thought and turn to go, wondering if you can possibly wait until morning.

Then you turn before you get to the foot of the stairs for one last look. This is the real Christmas. The tree shimmers

16

in beauty, the faint echo of a song drifts away; the stillness is awesome.

Tomorrow will be wonderfully exciting and full of laughter, but tonight belongs to the Christ Child. Your world is a near perfect thing and you can only say, "Thank you, oh thank you," before you turn and scamper off upstairs.

You lie in bed in an agony of excitement. You smother little shivers of ecstasy down inside. You can't sleep, you know you can't. Morning will never come, you can't sleep, you can't sleep, you can't sleep. And then someone is shaking you by the shoulder and Milt is saying in a loud whisper, "Wake up, Sleepy-head; it's morning!"

Then we're all up and dressing, the boys waiting on the slow girls. No one is permitted to go down alone. We were always quite scornful of children who were permitted to go down at any old hour and spoil things for the others.

We line up at the top of the steps. The youngest first, except for Martha who is given age preference because she carries the baby. My father gives the word and we start down. As we round the bend on the stairs, for one glorious moment it's all before us. What a thrill, that moment of sweet fulfillment! The stockings are in sight, the line breaks, it's Christmas! Merry, Merry Christmas!

fragments

Uncle Josh
───────

I never knew him by any other name than Uncle Josh. I knew him for only one day. I saw my mother look at Aunt Beth in a secretive way and say, "Uncle Josh is back!"

My aunt asked, "Riding the rails?" I didn't know what that meant, but to my eight-year-old mind it sounded exciting. I went right down to Grandfather's to find out.

Uncle Josh was sitting out by the barn. He was taller and leaner than anybody. His skin was the color of walnut stain which got on my hands when I helped Grandfather with the nuts in the Fall. Uncle Josh had lots of white hair and blue eyes that looked far away.

He said, "Hello, Sweetie." I liked that because no one had ever called me *Sweetie* especially not my brothers.

There were flat stones piled up against the barn where we could sit and lean up against the warm wood. I pulled my bare feet up onto the cool stone. He took my hand in his big rough one and we sat quietly for awhile just getting acquainted.

I asked him if he slept in the barn. He said, "I like the smell of hay and I hate to be closed in."

There was a shed across the alley from the barn where a row of sunflowers nodded in the hot sunshine. The soft buzz of insects filled the air. We could smell the barn, manure, leather, grain. It was not unpleasant, but earthy and homey.

"Did you ever see tumbleweeds?" he asked. "They grow in the plains and in the autumn they wither and blow about like great light balls. They travel for miles, wherever the wind blows them and plant seeds where farmers don't want them You can't catch them if you try."

fragments

"Did you try, Uncle Josh?"

"Many times!" he laughed.

"There's a place called Moose Head Lake," he continued. "The water is so crystal clear you can see the beautiful stones on the bottom. At night you can hear the weird, wild, eerie call of the loons. . . a primitive call that carries you back to ancient times."

Uncle Josh didn't talk like other people. I liked it. He made me think of things and places I'd never heard of before. I shivered and held tight to his hand.

It was quiet except for the horses moving about in their stalls and an occasional whinny.

"I know about a canyon so deep Indians live down at the bottom and grow fruit and vegetables. I rode all the way down on the back of a mule."

"Were you scared?"

"No reason to be scared. The mules are sure-footed, and it was such a sight! You'll ride down there someday. And on the north rim of the canyon the Kaibab squirrels live. They have bushy white tails. Few people ever get a glimpse of them, but I did."

"You were lucky, Uncle Josh."

"Can you believe trees so big a car can drive through them? Some of them are a thousand years old."

"How do you know about all these places?"

"Riding the rails," he answered. There it was again! He began saying words: Prairie du Chien, Dolly Sods, Fancy Gap, Woonsocket, Buckaloons, Ipperwash. I rolled the words around on my tongue. It was fun and we laughed and started all over again.

The sun was going down behind the barn and Uncle Josh thought my mother would be wanting me home for dinner. He said "Goodbye, Sweetie, keep wonder in your heart."

I was back at the barn first thing in the morning. Uncle

19

fragments

Josh was gone. I never saw him again, but I promised myself that one day when I grew up, I too would "ride the rails."

fragments

I Wonder What Happened to George

I wonder, what happened to George? There has always been a great mystery about my grandfather George Hartley. My father never talked about his family. My mother told us never to question him. When my brothers and sisters and I were together, we fantasized and made up wonderfully romantic stories about our grandfather.

We did learn a few things about our father's early life. When he was fifteen years old, his father died. Shortly after that he decided to go to East Palestine and look for a job. He sent his mother, his grandmother, and big sister ahead on the train. He borrowed a horse and wagon and, with his two younger brothers and all their possessions, made the trip from Salineville to East Palestine. It took most of a day. Arriving in East Palestine, he immediately got a job in the W.S. George Pottery. From that time on he took the entire responsibility of his family.

Before my father was thirty years old, his baby brother Johnny had died of meningitis; his brother Jim and sister Maud had died of tuberculosis.

We also learned that there had been a wealthy Uncle Abe whose heir was my grandfather with the stipulation that the entire estate would go from George to my father. Something happened and he was disinherited. This led to all sorts of speculations.

After my grandmother died at the age of eighty-eight, we went through her things hoping to find some clue concerning George. There were hundreds of postcards which we read carefully, but never a word about George. There were stacks of pictures, not one of George. One picture of Johnny sitting in a little red rocking chair on a

21

porch somewhere and one of Jim in a group of boys all wearing long funny bathing suits. There was no jewelry, no small keepsakes, nothing.

A few years after my parents died, my sister Lu and I decided to go to Salineville and find out about George Hartley.

Once when I was about nine years old, our father took us to Salineville to see the house that had been Uncle Abe's, the house that should have been ours. We intended to ride by and look at this wonderful house. As we drove past, a woman came out and waved. She invited us in. My father didn't seem upset or angry, as I remember. Mr. and Mrs. Hutson had inherited the house from Uncle Abe. They were distant cousins of my father.

Mrs. Hutson was round and jolly with very pink cheeks. She wore a starched apron tied around her ample middle. She laughed and hugged us, even my father. She smelled of ginger cookies and I loved her on the spot. Mr. Hutson was tall, had long white hair and the twinkliest blue eyes I had ever seen.

They insisted that we stay for dinner. It was as if they expected eight people to drop in. We sat in the kitchen at a big round table with a snowy white cloth. We had food I had never heard of. There was a dish of mashed potatoes with a mixture of lettuce, onions, vinegar, and bits of bacon on top. There was a dish of cucumbers and onions in sour cream and veal stew with big fluffy dumplings. There was smearcase and apple butter and apple pan dowdy. I didn't like everything, but I tried it all.

I must tell you about the house. It was huge and square, painted white with a blue roof. It had three stories with porches running around two sides of all three floors. I imagined the fun of leaning over the railing and calling down to someone on the second or first floor, or sending little messages up and down on strings. There were swings on each porch and chairs with fat blue cushions.

Outside there was a path that led to a springhouse. I didn't know what a springhouse was, but I wanted to find out. The path ran along beside a creek. It was dark and smelled of mold and leaves. The path sloped and I was afraid of falling off into the rushing water. Around the bend I saw a roof but no house. Then steps that led to nowhere. Mrs. Hutson came up the steps laughing. She told us to stoop and come on in. She opened a small door that she said always had to be kept locked. Inside, it was cool and dark. Brown crocks of milk sat on the dirt floor. She said when the cream came to the top she would skim it off and make butter. I stuck my finger in the crock and licked off the thick yellow cream.

My parents and the Hutsons sat on the porch and talked. They persuaded us to stay all night. Mrs. Hutson said we could explore all we wanted and while we were upstairs we could decide where we wanted to sleep. Up we scampered and looked in all the rooms and came back excited and puzzled. There weren't any beds! She laughed and shook all over. She went upstairs with us and went over to a tall chifforobe and said that was where my sister and I were going to sleep. I didn't see how we'd get much rest standing up. She pulled down the top and there was a bed all made up with plump white pillows. It was magic!

We left the Hutsons the next morning with promises to return and to keep in touch. We never did.

Years later my sister Lu and I drove past the house. It looked just the same, perhaps not as big as it had to a nine-year-old. There were the three porches just as I remembered. There wasn't any path to a springhouse, just a cleared field. The house was unoccupied; the name on the mailbox was one we didn't recognize.

We decided to go to the courthouse in Lisbon, Ohio to find some history of George Hartley: a birth certificate, a marriage license, births of children. In Lisbon, we learned that all records before 1900 had been destroyed by fire.

Our next stop was the cemetery. The caretaker there had no record of graves of that period. He leaned on a tombstone and rambled on about lack of money to keep records and graves in shape. But he did tell us about an old woman who lived in Waterford, a few miles from there. She might know something about our relatives since she was nearing a hundred years old and had lived in this part of Ohio all her life.

We found Mary Chain in the little town of Waterford in a small blue house perched on top of a hill. We wondered how she ever managed the sixteen steps up to her tall house. She was sitting on the porch looking like a tiny sparrow all in black, save for a starched white handkerchief around her neck and pinned with a lovely brooch.

Yes, she had known Mattie and George Hartley, she said. They always seemed like a nice young couple. They moved away a long time ago, about the time the oldest boy was fifteen or sixteen. She believed George had died. She thought he was an itinerant preacher. She kept rocking and trying to remember. She shook her head and smiled, her pale watery eyes not seeing us at all. We left quietly. We hoped we hadn't upset her.

We came home not knowing any more about George than before. We hadn't learned anything dishonorable about him or anything especially good either. It was as if he had never lived, had a mother, a wife, four children, and a little farm. Why was he disinherited? Was it over some silly argument or was it something illegal? Did my father actually not know what happened, only fifteen at the time? Did my grandmother never talk about her husband, the father of her children? Did he leave home on one of his trips and never return? Did he die in disgrace, alone and far from his family? Or did he indeed die peacefully in his bed at home? With the death of her husband and her three children in such a short time was she so traumatized that she put it out of her mind, into yesterday, into last year, into forever?

Now my children make up stories, sometimes romantic, sometimes sinister, and I still wonder what happened to George.

fragments

Remember Charlie

I think it was that summer at Mentor-on-the-Lake when I decided that one day I would live on the shores of Lake Erie. It took me twenty years.

The July my family rented a cottage there, my cousins rented one next door. Six children in each family made every day a hectic celebration.

My soul mate was Pinkie. Each morning at dawn we sneaked out to take a dip in the lake. How chilly those early mornings were! We watched the sunrise, walked carefully on pristine sand, lay on our backs in the blue infinity of the lake and looked at endless sky. Nothing has ever been better than that.

There was a little store, strictly off limits, where they sold Boston Coolers. We decided to risk the wrath of my father and headed for the store. It was cool and dark inside, smelled of cigarettes, medicine, ice cream, and peanuts. It was crowded with men and boys laughing and shoving each other around. It was scary! At the back of the store were little round tables with glass tops displaying pictures of perch and pickerel and bass.

We got our Boston Coolers (ten cents each) in tall green glasses and carried them carefully to the last table. Oh! How delicious! Two scoops of ice cream filled to the brim with ginger ale. How smugly we looked at each other. Suddenly the door opened and who should come in but my father. We were paralyzed with fright. He looked right at us for an interminable moment. His expression just barely changed. Then he made his purchase and left. He never, ever said a word.

There was one abominable thing that summer. The

chemical toilet! We had to get psyched-up to the ordeal and, when it wasn't possible to wait any longer, we'd hold our breath, and dash in while the other one stood guard outside. We'd come out gasping for air. Later on trips, my mother said Pinkie and I could wait longer than any kids she'd ever known. I attribute this dubious honor to Mentor-on-the-Lake and the chemical toilet.

A group of young men had a cottage down the beach from us. On mornings when they jogged past they'd holler, "Hello!"

We'd giggle and run the other way.

"I'm Charlie," one boy yelled. "Who are you?"

"We're Pinkie and Billie," we answered. After that, someone always shouted, "Hello, Pinkie and Billie!" And we'd laugh and yell, "Hello, Charlie!"

Later on I'd look at Pinkie and say, "Remember Charlie." And Pinkie would laugh and look secretive.

Evenings were magic. The moon over the lake was breathtaking. It left miles wide streaks of silver. Away off in the distance we could hear faint music from a merry-go-round, "K K K Katie, Beautiful Katie."

How marvelous the memory of that long ago summer.

Cats Aren't Rattlesnakes

"I'd like a cat. Cats are neat," Michael told his friend Charlie. "But my mom hates cats. She acts like they're rattlesnakes."

"Maybe if she knew a cat personally, she'd change her mind," Charlie said.

"Aw, it wouldn't do any good. Once, a cat rubbed against her legs and she almost had hysterics."

"Maybe they'll get you a dog. Aren't they taking you out to the dog kennels on Sunday?"

"Yeah, they have it all figured out. They think I'll forget all about cats."

"What do you see in cats anyway? They aren't even friendly."

"That's why I like them. They're independent. They don't grovel around begging you to like them. They don't care if you like them or not. Nobody pushes them around!" Michael's eyes sparkled defiantly.

"Take it easy!" Charlie said. "I could get you a good cat for nothing."

"Yeah, but my dad says: 'a boy's best friend,' and all that rot!"

"Well, good luck! You usually get what you want. 'Spoiled rotten,' that's what I always say. What do you always say?"

"I say 'quit goofing off!' I'll let you know how it turns out. Come over Sunday night."

Charlie got up off the floor where he had been doing a few pushups. "So long, see you Sunday."

Michael enjoyed the ride into the country. It was a fine good-to-be-alive day. He was optimistic about getting a cat.

fragments

They arrived at a big country place, all trees and streams and tall grass and lovely hiding places for cats.

A woman hustled out the front door. "I'm Mrs. Smallwood. Tain't my job to look after the dogs, but my man's not here. Look around. We've got lots of dogs."

They had dogs! Big dogs, long dogs, yippy dogs, quiet dogs- all perfectly good dogs.

"Pick one out Michael. I'm sure you'll get to be pals in no time," his mother said.

He scuffed his feet in the dirt and kicked a stone as he walked out past the last kennel.

Suddenly he let out a yell, "Yippee! They have a bunch of cats!"

He saw a silver-gray Persian kitten with amazing turquoise- blue eyes.

"This has gotta be my cat. He walked right up to me. Can't you see? He picked me."

"You know how I hate cats. Maybe he isn't for sale," his mother said hopefully.

"Is he for sale? Please, is he for sale?" asked Michael.

"Well, I wouldn't want just anyone to have him," Mrs Smallwood said.

"You'll never be sorry if you sell him to me," said Michael as he picked up his cat.

"I've named him Oliver," Michael said on the way home. "He looks like an Oliver."

"What does an Oliver look like?" his father asked.

"Like somebody-not just any old alley cat. A V.I.P. cat."

"Where's this marvelous cat?" Charlie yelled, when he came over.

"Open the refrigerator door. If he thinks there's food he'll be here in a flash."

As Oliver came dashing into the room at the sound of

29

food, Michael's mother hurriedly left the room.

"That's a weird cat you've got," Charlie said. "You can't get away with anything."

"Just smart that's all. A super cat!"

"Your mother hates him, doesn't she?"

"Yeah, she does. She's afraid of cats."

In January, the family went on a vacation to visit Michael's grandparents. They took Oliver to stay with Ginny Wing, his mother's friend.

"I'll take good care of him," Ginny said. "See you Sunday."

Three days later a frantic Ginny met them at the door. "He's gone," she said tearfully. "My neighbor came to the door. She didn't know about Oliver, and he just flew out. We've hunted every place. It's my fault!"

Michael's mother was very quiet. She didn't say she hated cats.

They asked at each house along the street. They looked in vacant lots. They called his name over and over. They hunted until it was too dark to see. The next day, they ran an ad in the paper- nothing.

"He isn't used to being out," Michael said sadly. "He sleeps in my room and he loves to sit by the fire."

After two weeks of cold, wet weather Michael gave up. His mother didn't once say she hated cats.

On Friday afternoon, she picked Michael up after school to walk the few blocks to Ginny's house. He was carrying his books and his clarinet. He started calling in a monotonous little voice "Here, Oliver, here, Oliver!" not really expecting any results.

Suddenly he yelled, "There's a cat, a gray cat! I think it's Oliver!"

He ran across the wet field toward the cat. His mother let out a screech and beat him to it. She grabbed up the bedraggled cat. Sure enough, it was Oliver! All wet and full of burrs and half-starved. He was shivering and crying. He snuggled down contentedly in her arms.

Michael started to say that he'd carry Oliver if she'd carry his books. Then he smiled and didn't say a word.

That night at supper Michael's father asked innocently, "Who picked Oliver up and carried him all the way to Ginny's house?"

His mother said in a surprised voice, "Why- I did!" Just then Oliver came in waving his tail majestically and Michael said, "I'm so glad Mom brought you home, Oliver!"

His mother smiled happily. Michael and his father exchanged looks, eyes twinkling. His mother remembered to say, almost too late, "I hate cats!"

fragments

The Willow Touch

Two scraggly little gray kittens came to live at my daughter's house sixteen years ago. Five-year-old Matt chose the striped one and named him-what else? Stripes. Andrea took the other one and named him, quite aptly, Pussy Willow.

Stripes was the bolder of the two and less friendly. At first he led Pussy Willow into a great deal of mischief. But being cats of great intelligence, they soon learned the ways and habits of well brought up felines and simply made the house their own particular domain.

I was never a great cat lover myself and ignored them as best I could. But every time I entered the mud room, they greeted me with a meow simply saying, "Hello." It wasn't long before I was hooked. I looked forward to their greeting and if they weren't around, I asked where they were.

Stripes slept with Matt and Willow with Andrea. The cats had their own baskets and my daughter pretended they were snugly in their beds. As soon as the lights were out, the two streaked upstairs to nestle down beside a child. When they went outside to parade around the garden, Stripes went ahead and Willow followed along behind. They snooped into everything like a couple of old ladies intent on picking up bits of gossip to talk over later.

By this time the cats were part of the family and had the run of the house. They never got into too much trouble. They could walk daintily around fragile vases without breaking them.

When I'd sit at the bar in the kitchen, Willow would jump up beside me on the other stool and keep me company. He didn't beg for food, just sat in friendly

32

companionship.

When Stripes was about eight years old, he went for a walk alone. He never came back. Matt was devastated, but after that, Willow belonged to both of them.

When Andrea went off to college, Willow wandered around hunting for her. He sat on her bed and cried. Then he transferred his sleeping place to Matt's room.

Even though the cats belonged to the kids, they were, in reality, their mother Eileen's cats. After all, she fed them, filled their bowls with water, took care of the litter box, and took them to the vet. And then there were times when the kids were in school

When my husband Bill was there, Willow liked nothing better than to curl up on his lap. As they sat in front of the fire on a cold winter evening, they were contented for hours.

Then it was time for Matt to go off to college, and Willow was left with Eileen and her husband, Bob. Bob had, at first, pretended to dislike cats, but he was soon doing little things for Willow. My daughter, Eileen, had a high shelf in the mud room filled with flowers, and Willow liked to sit up there surrounded by leafy ferns and look out the window. Bob had a fan put in the mud room to make it more comfortable for Willow.

In summer, Willow loved to sit under the apple tree and look out over the wild flower garden, or tiptoe on the stone path amid the blossoms and put a soft paw out to touch.

The summer Willow was sixteen, he became quite thin. He no longer scampered to his dish for food. His eyes were dull and he couldn't jump up on the stool to keep us company. A trip to the vet was in order.

Back home, Eileen called me. The doctor had to put Willow to sleep. She was distraught. She had brought him home and was going to bury him under the apple tree in the flower garden. I went up to be with her. She was digging in hard clay; I helped. We put Willow in a box. He looked to be asleep, all curled up, white paws up to his face. We touched the soft gray fur. We remembered how funny he'd been, how many times we'd laughed at his antics, how he'd hated his bath and his collar, and how many years he'd been with us. She told me how he had purred as she held him for the last time.

Two grown women standing in the backyard crying over a cat! But it wasn't just a cat. It was Willow we had lost.

fragments

On Glamour

I read this article about being glamorous. One thing it stated is of the utmost importance. The absolute must that makes all the difference is that you should hold your rib cage high.

Well, it's really pitiful what happens to my rib cage, especially when I'm at the top of a twenty foot ladder painting the peak of the garage. I'm wearing a pair of beat-up shorts and one of Bill's old shirts. After four hours of this I can hardly hold up the bucket (paint bucket) let alone my rib cage.

But after all, I want to hold my husband as well as the next gal (her own husband), and there is plenty of time to think and get a new perspective on things up there. This rib cage thing may be just the thing that will pay off.

So when I see my husband at the foot of the ladder, briefcase in hand, well-groomed and debonair, I hold my rib cage high and slowly descend. I look my beloved squarely in the eye, and he says, "What's the matter? Can't you breathe?"

I heard that velvet really turns a man on, especially black velvet. With that in mind, I went to the local boutique and bought a black velvet dress. My husband was taking me out to dinner and I planned a dramatic entrance. I descended the stairs slowly in my seductive velvet dress, a simple strand of pearls, nylons, high heels, and a touch of Arpege in all the right places. My husband looked up from his paper, patted me companionably on the behind and said, "I've always liked you in that dress!"

My husband believes in fun. He believes in having one hell of a good time. "You're only here once" he says, "and

35

by golly, you may as well enjoy yourself."

He's a peach of a guy, a dandy fellow, and he means every word of it. But he believes all this should start to happen after the work is finished.

For twenty years, he has been telling me that we are almost caught up; that it's almost time for the fun to start. I believe him. That happy thought has helped me through many a task.

At first, I dreamed about dancing in some sophisticated, far-off place with simply divine music. I saw myself beautifully turned out in a simple sheath, rib cage held high. Men perked up as I danced gracefully around the floor, adored by my tall handsome husband.

Or I was on a stretch of sandy beach, gorgeously tanned, wearing a white bathing suit. All eyes followed me as I strolled by, and there were gasps of amazement at my superb swimming. (At the time I was taking lessons at the Y.)

I leafed through magazines and looked at shorts, pale sandals, sun-drenched coves, little beach coats, bare legs, and wind-blown hair. I was intrigued with off-the-beaten-path places, with walking through France, bicycle tours, and tramp steamers.

But gradually I found myself looking up guided tours, something worthwhile and educational. Six weeks with thirty other people who wanted something worthwhile and educational. I became interested in basic traveling dresses, comfortable shoes, and light-weight girdles.

Lately, however, my mind seems to linger over something loose and comfortable, lots of goodies, and a quiet game of pinochle. I was wondering, do you prefer chocolates or mixed nuts?

Our Time

It was Christmas 1988. In the morning, we had a wonderful time just being together again. We had opened our presents and enjoyed a late breakfast. We were visiting our son Michael and his wife Lorraine in Jacksonville, North Carolina. Their two teenage children, Adam and Susan, were home for the holidays. Michael and Lorraine were busy preparing the feast we were to enjoy later. Because the kids were home and friends were in and out all the time, we were staying in a motel just a few blocks from their house.

My husband Bill was tired from the long drive from Ohio the day before. He decided to go back to the Onslow Inn for a nap.

"Be sure and be here by five o'clock for dinner!" Lorraine called.

"Oh, I wouldn't miss that for anything!" Bill responded. About four-thirty, I called the motel to make sure he was awake.

The manager answered the phone. "I just heard him driving out," he said.

"That's good, he must be hungry."

By five o'clock he hadn't arrived.

"Maybe he stopped for gas, or had some shopping to do," Michael said "He'll be along any minute."

"On Christmas Day?" That seemed odd.

By five-thirty he still hadn't arrived. I called the motel again. I thought he might have gone back for something.

The manager went to the room and checked. "He isn't in the room. The luggage is all there; the car is gone."

By this time, we were extremely worried. At six o'clock

we called the police. They got the license number, color, and make of car and said they'd look for him.

At seven, we were in a panic and trying very hard to tell each other everything would be all right. We called the police again. He said he had all available men on the lookout for the car.

A few minutes later a patrolman came to the door. He was a tall, nice-looking man who was very kind and seemed to care about finding Bill. He assured us there had been no accidents and no crimes reported.

"Describe your husband," he said.

"He's six feet tall, gray hair," I said.

"What was he wearing?"

"Blue slacks, white shirt, blue tie, blue sweater."

"Does he wear glasses?"

"Yes, and he was wearing a blue cap."

"How much money was he carrying?"

"About four hundred dollars."

"Social Security number?" "I don't know."

"Wristwatch? Any jewelry?"

"Yes, a watch, no other jewelry."

"If he is lost, will he pull over and park the car and wait for help or just ride around?"

"Ride around," I said. "I'm sure he'd just ride around."

"Do you have a picture of him?"

Michael found a snapshot that he had taken recently.

"I'll run this on television later tonight if we haven't found him. Also, on local stations in Ohio where you live. Maybe he started for home for some reason."

Meantime, Adam and some of his friends rode around the city, but no one was able to spot the car. Michael and I rode around also, but soon decided that, in all the traffic, it was impossible. So we went back to sit by the phone.

By this time the turkey dinner was on hold. No one

wanted to eat anything, but Lorraine thought we'd better try; maybe it would take our minds off things and make waiting easier.

"I'm not eating Christmas dinner without Grandpa!" Adam said.

We persuaded him to come to the table.

"Will you please say the blessing, Susan?" Michael asked.

Susan said the usual "Bless this food" and then added, "Please, God, show Grandpa how to get home!"

As she finished speaking, the clock struck nine-thirty.

Meanwhile at a small store on the other side of town, a woman was about to close for the night. She usually closed earlier, but for some reason she didn't quite understand, she waited. It was just past nine-thirty when a man drove in and asked to use the phone.

At the table we nervously tried to eat. The phone rang. For an instant, the whole world stopped. Was he alive? Please, God, make it good news! Lorraine jumped up to answer. Then we heard her laughing. "Bill! Where are you? Are you all right? Stay right there, don't move. We'll come and get you."

"Who's going?" Adam asked.

"Father, you go and take Grandma," Susan said.

"I'm going," Lorraine said, grabbing her coat.

"Well, I don't think we should all go, it will just scare Grandpa,'" Adam said.

"I'll stay," Susan said.

But as we started out the door they both came running out.

"We want to go!" We all piled into the car and found the little store. There he was standing beside the car waiting for us, smiling that wonderful smile of his.

Bill didn't know what happened. He woke up, got in the car, and started to drive. He couldn't remember where he was or where I was, but he had to find me. He had been

39

driving around all that time, had put 150 miles on the car. He remembered being in Morehead City. Suddenly, he looked up and saw a sign that said Jacksonville, and he remembered that was where Michael lived. He had to get to a phone and call him. So, he pulled into the little store.

The patrolman came back to the house to see that everything was all right. He was genuinely pleased that Bill was home. He said it didn't always turn out so well. He shook hands with us and wished us all a Merry Christmas. I can't say enough about the courteous and caring men of the Jacksonville, North Carolina police force.

Later, our doctor said the loss of memory was probably due to a new kind of medicine Bill had started to take to alleviate the pain in his leg which had been injured during the war. That, and waking up suddenly in a strange place and being overly tired. But we were to be alert to it ever happening again. It never has.

Nine-thirty must have been our time. As though it were a gift, the store stayed open past nine-thirty. Susan's prayer came at nine-thirty and Bill, suddenly, right at nine-thirty, saw the sign.

fragments

Designs

I push the wheelchair down the corridor to the wide windows.

He likes to look at the jet streams across the sky.

"Was it fun flying those big planes?" I ask.

"I liked it. It was better than anything you can imagine, but not all the time. It was great when I transported supplies, but when I brought out the wounded, it wasn't so great. Actually, it's more fun flying small planes, then you're part of the sky," Bill answered.

Here comes Rudy, another veteran, in his motorized chair. He wants company. He pulls up close to us, gets his harmonica out of his pocket and plays *Let Me Call You Sweetheart* and then right into the *Beer Barrel Polka*. He's really quite good.

"Do you remember how we used to dance the polka?" I ask.

"I don't remember," Bill says.

"You were such a good dancer. Don't you remember how we could whirl around the floor?"

"I don't remember."

I have this thing about hands. I think you can tell a lot about a person by looking at his hands. When I think of my father, I can see his hands clearly- strong, capable, well-kept nails. Now I look at his hands, artist's hands, caressing hands.

"I washed the car today," I say brightly.

"You should have waited. I would have helped you. It's too hard for you to do all by yourself."

"Oh, it wasn't bad. It didn't take long at all."

"You can't reach the top."

41

"I stood on a chair."

"I'll help next time," and he pats my hand.

Tommy is coming down the hall, lured by the sound of music. He pushes the chair with his feet. He has very small feet black shoes, white socks. They all wear white socks. He comes very slowly. It takes forever. He parks his chair close, touching the others. He doesn't talk, just smiles all the time. I smile back. He keeps time to the music with his feet.

Rudy puts his harmonica away. "I used to be a cook in the army," he says. "I could cook better meals than they have here."

I have heard it before.

The nurse comes down the hall with medicines. She asks if I've been to the exhibit of pottery in the auditorium. She thinks maybe there is something there I would like to see.

"Do you have something in the show?" I ask him.

"I don't remember."

"You've been going to activities every day, haven't you?"

"I don't remember," he says looking puzzled, trying to remember.

"Maybe you have something in the show."

"I don't think so. I don't remember."

Now it's time for lunch and I push his wheelchair down to his assigned table in the dining room. Rudy and Tommy follow behind.

"What's for lunch?" I ask.

"Pork chops, mashed potatoes, green beans, applesauce, tomatoes, and for dessert, caramel pudding." The orderly laughs.

"Sounds pretty good to me." He goes off down the hall.

"Aren't you eating?" Bill asks.

"No, I have errands."

"Do you have enough money?"

"I have plenty of money."

"How long will you be gone?"

"Not long."

"When will you be back?"

"Maybe tomorrow." I pat his shoulder kiss him softly, and leave.

As I pass the nurses' station, Linda says "No one is there now, but the auditorium is still open. You'd better look in at the exhibit."

"I don't really think Bill has anything in the show."

I go down the corridor to the elevators. The auditorium is across the hall. I pause at the door, decide whether to go on. Oh well, I may as well take a look since I'm here.

I push open the heavy double doors. On a long table the full length of the room is a display of pottery. In the center on a table covered with black velvet is a ginger jar. It is about twelve inches tall, pale lustrous greenish-gold with delicate designs in brown. On a small card propped against the vase is his name.

I stand beside the ginger jar and weep.

Picnic

My older sister Lu wants to see our brother Charlie one more time. She lives in a rest home about one hundred miles away. I don't know if I can pull it off, but I know a picnic is the only way to avoid well-intentioned nurses and social workers.

Charlie lives in a rest home a few miles from me and can travel, but he can't eat in a restaurant because he has to be fed.

My youngest sister Ginny and her husband Chet can come if they take their time and stay with me a couple of days before. They live several miles away. Chet can't drive anymore. Ginny is a good driver. All she has to do is persuade Chet to make the trip.

We choose a beautiful fall day, bright sun, warm breeze, not a cloud in the sky. My husband Bill is driving. He's a great driver, used to teach Drivers' Education at the high school. He can't help much with the walking because be walks with a cane and quite slowly. Bill has had multiple sclerosis for a good many years, half his lifetime.

We arrive at the rest home early to pick up Charlie. He's all ready, dressed in his good clothes and a warm sweater. The nurses like him.

"I hear you're going to see your big sister," one of the nurses calls.

"Have a good time, Charlie." An old woman in a wheelchair pulls up beside us. "Take me along, Charlie."

Charlie laughs. "Can't do it. We're going on a picnic. Haven't been on a picnic for years."

"This is my little sister Ginny," he tells the nurses. "She's here from New York. Isn't she a doll? We used to call her

44

Apple Blossom. She was so cute."

"That was a while ago," Ginny says, laughing. "I haven't heard that in years."

We help Charlie into the car. He sits in the front seat with Bill. Turning around, he holds out his hand to Chet. "Glad you could make it, Chet. Great to see you."

"Wouldn't have missed it. Seems like old times."

It takes two hours to drive to rest home number two. Charlie enjoys the ride. He had worked for a lumber company once and now is especially interested in new houses. And once he had sold barn equipment and drawn blueprints for barns. This very old part of Ohio had been part of his territory. We go near a town where Charlie used to live before he became ill and was left alone.

When we get to the old farmhouse, we see Lu sitting on the porch in her wheelchair. Her daughter Debbie is with her. Debbie has Down syndrome and lives with her mother. They have one room and their own bath. The room is small, so they can reach out and touch each other's hands from their beds. Debbie works at a sheltered workshop five days a week. She takes the bus every morning at eight and returns at four. Sometimes she gets off the bus crying. When you ask her what is wrong, she doesn't know. She has a friend at the workshop, the only friend her age.

Lu is tied in the wheelchair with a white towel. To me she will always be my beautiful older sister. When I hear *Pomp and Circumstance*, I can see her coming across the campus dressed as Cinderella in filmy white with a silver crown on her head; the flowers and lake and trees are a fitting background for a May Queen.

I untie the towel that holds her in the chair.

A nurse cries out in alarm, "You can't take her out of the wheelchair. She can't walk. She'll just fall."

"No wheelchair allowed," I sing out.

"How are you going to get her in the car?" Her crisp

white dress rustles as she walks. She sounds cross.

"She's going to walk," I answer.

"Oh, I do want to walk. I haven't walked in such a long time," Lu says.

The nurse is resigned. She pats Lu's shoulder, "Well, have a good time, dear. You too, Debbie."

Ginny gets on one side, I on the other. Lu is as light as a feather. "Look at me, Debbie! I'm walking. I'm doing pretty good. I'm walking."

Debbie trails along behind. We get Lu into the car, buckle her into the back seat. Debbie gets in the middle. She sees Charlie in the front seat. She's crazy about Charlie. She leans forward and starts singing in a childish treble, "I love you a bushel and a peck," and Charlie chimes in with, "You bet your pretty neck I do."

Chet is beside Debbie. I'll ride in front between Bill and Charlie. Ginny, being the youngest, volunteers to get in the back of the station wagon. She gets in, we close the door and she starts to scream, "Let me out; let me out! I can't stand it in here!" So, I trade places with her. The back of the wagon is not high enough to sit up, so I half sit and half lean into the back seat so I won't miss anything. We have only ten miles to go.

Chet looks back and says, "How is it back there?"

I say. "Just like downtown," and for no reason at all, we start to laugh.

We laugh until our eyes fill with tears and when we get settled down someone says, "Just like downtown," and we're off again.

We reach the park and find a nice green table. We get everyone settled, Debbie beside Charlie. I get the food out of the car. I have things everyone can handle, plenty of small sandwiches, gallons of lemonade, and chips. Best of all a huge chocolate sheet cake cut in small easily handled pieces.

"These are the best ham salad sandwiches I've ever tasted. You're such a good cook, Wilma. I'll take another one please," Lu says.

Debbie claps her hands and says in her sweet childish voice, "Oh, chocolate cake! I love chocolate cake. Don't you, Mama, don't you just love Wilma's chocolate cake?"

"How are you doing, Charlie?" Ginny asks. She has been helping him.

"Just hand me two more, and a few more chips."

More lemonade for everyone.

"This is a wonderful meal," Lu says.

It is a golden afternoon with bright leaves floating softly down upon the table. A puff of breeze turns the undersides of the leaves to silver, and Lu says, in a soft voice, "Grow old along with me, the best is yet to be, the last of life for which the first is made."

The silence is complete.

Then Charlie says, "That's a crock!"

We look up, startled. Then we start to laugh. We rock back and forth. We pound our fists on the table. We laugh until we are exhausted. We get quiet for a minute, then Chet says, "Just like downtown," and it starts all over again.

Finally, everyone is silent. We look into each other's eyes held together by a fragile thread of memories. We think of our brother Jim so far away. We think of our parents and our brother and sister gone so long ago. There used to be nine. Now there are five.

"Let's sing," Ginny says. It breaks that thin line between joy and sorrow.

Charlie starts in his deep voice, "When the saints come marching in when the saints come marching in..."

We all join in. What matter that we aren't quite in tune? What matter that our voices quaver and we can't remember the words? It's a golden day and we are survivors.

Book II

Along the Way

fragments

The Camping Trip

"I wouldn't even consider taking seven kids on a vacation! It's out of the question!" My father laid down the law.

Mother had other ideas and she continued to work on it. Finally she suggested we could go on a camping trip. Father, rather reluctantly, agreed.

Then, as if it had been his idea all along, he bought a tent and we put it up in the back yard for a trial run. It was a wonderful tent! About twelve feet square, big enough for all six of us to lie across the back. My parents would sleep on cots at the entrance. There were windows on each side covered with netting that could be opened and closed by pulling little cords. A flap at the front made a sort of porch for the two cots, a small folding table and a two-burner stove.

My mother bought a bolt of blue and gray cotton material at Sears and made pajamas for all of us. We wore khaki camping clothes, the girls knickers and middies, the boys short pants and shirts. I had a ridiculous straw hat, blue and red, triangular--reminiscent of George Washington. It had tassels on each side. I loved that hat and wore it all the time.

We each had one change of clothes for dressing up, underwear for each day, and our bathing suits, all in a huge box strapped to the top of the Studebaker along with the tent.

The Sutherns went with us. Mr. Suthern owned a drug store beside my father's hardware store. They had been friends for many years and his wife, Bess, was Mother's friend. They had two daughters, Grace and Ellen whom we secretly

51

thought were wimps. They were both blond and blue-eyed, played with dolls and never, never got dirty. Mrs. Suthern was a small round woman with fly-away hair, wide blue eyes and a look of helplessness about her that kept her from doing much work and assured her the company of men hovering around to help. Mr. Suthern was small and full of energy, always eager to help his "three girls". They adored him. I think they saw him as ten feet tall.

We were headed for Port Huron, Michigan. One of Dad's salesmen was always inviting us to visit him. He owned a grove of Birch trees on the shore of Lake Huron. When he heard about our camping trip he said we could camp there as long as we wanted.

We started early in the morning and would camp someplace the first night and reach Port Huron the next day. The Sutherns would stay at a hotel the first night.

The Sutherns followed us in their small Ford. Grace and Ellen sat primly in the back seat wearing matching pink dresses and little hats with ribbons, and holding dolls. In our Studebaker we would zoom up the hills then wait for them at the top. Then we would yell smart-alecky things at them and their car. If we got too insulting my father would threaten to turn around and go home.

Everyone who passed our car smiled and waved. My father thought it was because we had an Ohio license and Michigan was just a very friendly state. But finally he got suspicious and stopped the car to check things out. We kids had written a sign that we held at the back window that read, "Smile if you think we're cute."

Dad threatened to turn around and go home.

There were no actual campgrounds, we just looked for a good place, stopped and asked permission to put up our tent for one night. About sunset we came to a small orchard beside a well-kept white farmhouse. It looked like a perfect place. Dad went to the door to ask permission. A big handsome woman came out and said her name was Mrs. Hoffenmeyer. She talked to Dad, then came out to the car to check out mother and all of us kids. She laughed a lot and was amazed at so many kids in one family on a camping trip. We evidently passed inspection because she said we were welcome to stay, and she said we could use the bathroom in her basement, she would leave the basement door open for us.

In the morning we stopped to say thank you to Mrs. Hoffenmeyer. Dad offered to pay for the use of the orchard, but she didn't want any money. She said she'd never had so much fun, she had sat up most of the night watching us with her binoculars. She kept laughing and said the little boys had not bothered to use the facilities. It made the boys embarrassed and kinda mad. But I thought it was funny.

She had coffee for Mother and Dad, milk for us kids and doughnuts for everyone. She insisted she didn't want any money, but I saw Dad put something in her apron pocket.

By mid-afternoon we arrived in Port Huron. The silver-yellowish Birch trees were an open woods letting sunlight filter through to clumps of wild flowers and strange tall grasses, the ground sloping down to a sandy beach and the blue waters of Lake Huron. It was a magic place.

We set up camp not far from the shore and the Sutherns pitched their smaller tent about thirty feet from ours. Between the tents we had a picnic table and a ring of blackened stones with stacked wood nearby. Dad tied a rope between two trees, halfway between our tents and hung up a kerosene lantern. Here we could run and play freely among the trees, swim or play in the sand. It was quite safe.

I remember after supper we would go down to the lake with a cake of ivory soap for a bath, then into our striped pajamas. Now we could sit around the campfire and listen to the stories our parents had to tell. Within that circle of light it was all love and laughter.

53

fragments

But beyond the perimeter of light, the trees suddenly became menacing; we knew all sorts of wild and dangerous things roamed the forest. Big black bears with small beady eyes scrunch behind trees, then silently come out and hunt little kids. Sometimes we could hear strange sounds above the soft lapping of waves, a crunch of footsteps dragging through sand or a kind of shuffle on the ground. I pushed shivers way down inside and held my arms tight around myself.

When the fire dies down we are sent to bed. I lie awake for a long time. I can hear my mother and father talking and laughing quietly with the Sutherns. I can hear them preparing to come to bed, Mother getting settled on her cot, Father's quiet goodnight. Then he turns off the kerosene lamp, only the faint glimmer of his flashlight is visible. He gets settled on his cot and turns off his light. It is dark! It is pitch black!

Lying there with my brothers and sisters, hearing the soft lapping of waves and knowing my mother and father are just outside the tent, I know we are safe. I know no bears can possibly get us.

fragments

Beyond the Grape Arbor

I could run faster than any eleven-year-old in the neighborhood, and I could hit a ball just as far. I couldn't see any reason why I shouldn't belong to the boys' baseball team. I'd been a kibitzer for a whole season and I noticed the boys were beginning to have private discussions about what to do with me or rather how to get rid of me. After huddles and arguments and a few choice words from Mother to quit squabbling or quit playing, they realized they were facing a crucial situation. The decision was made. I was to be a fielder. I knew what that was; you had to catch the ball. I thought that would lead to promotions and I would probably be permitted to bat at some later date or be president of the ball club.

Our backyard was divided about two-thirds of the way by a dense grape arbor. The ballpark, such as it was, was on the larger side. As fielder the boys placed me beyond the grape arbor. In the unlikely event that a ball was ever batted across the grape arbor, my job was to find it and throw it back immediately. The boys explained all that as they grinned and looked at each other with looks that said all too clearly, "We've sure put
one over on her!"

Mother was happy. The game resumed. I was satisfied that at last I was on the team. Standing out there beyond the grape arbor it was hard to know what was going on. After awhile I became bored. I sneaked in the house and got a book, settled myself on the grass in my assigned place and started to read. I lost all track of time, the game went on and on. Games only ended when it was too dark to play.

Suddenly right out of the blue a fast ball came sailing over the grape arbor and landed in my two hands as I sat there holding my book. Quick as a flash I yelled and threw that sucker up and away over the grape arbor. Someone caught it on the other side. The boys screamed and yelled and I knew that being a fielder was a very important part of the team.

I'm sorry to report that it never actually led to any other position but it didn't really matter. It wasn't long before I looked at the boys in a different light.

fragments

Fancy Work Club

It was an exciting day for us when Mother had Fancy Work Club. She entertained the ladies once a year. I remember one particular time. It was all hustle and bustle and the whole house was practically turned upside down with cleaning, airing and decorating. You'd think the ladies would stay in one room, but they didn't. One by one or maybe two by two they had to use the upstairs bathroom and this gave them a chance to peek into the bedrooms. While downstairs they could always offer to help with the lunch. There you are! The whole house had to be immaculate so nobody could later exclaim; "Did you see the boys' bedroom!"

The boys were sent off to my grandmother's which was just down the street. My two sisters and I wore our Sunday clothes. I wore my blue silk dress, a blue ribbon on my short hair, knee socks and patent leather shoes. I don't remember what my sisters wore, but I know they both had long braids down their backs with bright ribbons. My mother wore her gray silk skirt that had a wide crushed belt of the same material. She wore a pink blouse that my father had given her. On birthdays and holidays he usually gave her a blouse and he liked her in pink with lace or some sort of embroidery. With her dark hair piled high on her head, a few stray curls escaping I thought she was the prettiest lady there.

The scented ladies started arriving about 2:00. They hung their coats in the vestibule that was a room about eight feet square with a stained glass window, a bench on one side where you could sit and remove your overshoes. Along one side was a row of hooks for coats. Later on, my sisters and I would go into the vestibule and touch the fur coats, try on the hats and admire the kid gloves.

fragments

Our house had a library where we were all allowed to play. Here there were books, games, and good sturdy furniture. Opening off of this was the living room. This room was off limits. It was about thirty feet long and almost as wide. The floor was covered with a blue velvet carpet. A huge blue and rose colored sofa was in front of the fireplace. There were two chairs to match. They had big chunky arms and were wonderful to sit in. A long mahogany table was behind the sofa with a velvet runner and a set of small leather books. At one end was the upright piano with our violins on top. In the corner beside the piano was a big black leather chair. When you sat in that chair you felt wrapped around and safe. Although we didn't play in that room, I loved to go in there by myself, cover up with the blue Indian blanket, because it was always cool in there, and take my favorite book and an apple. Under the fringed lamp I could read for hours.

At the windows the blue and rose curtains matched the furniture. The walls were pale blue and my father had the local artist stencil a border around the walls next to the ceiling. An oak staircase led up to the second floor. It was seldom used because there was another staircase that went up from the kitchen,

When Mother had Fancy Work Club, the French doors were opened and here the ladies sat and did fancy work. They crocheted lace on handkerchiefs, embroidered pillow cases, knit Afghans or tatted. I was intrigued by the little ivory shuttle that went in and out making delicate lace. One lady was embroidering flowers on a lunch cloth. There was a great deal of teasing because she evidently had been bringing the same cloth for years. I think they did more talking than working.

Mrs. Logan was a big heavy lady who wore unusual dresses and a great deal of jewelry. My mother said she went to New York to buy her clothes. She wore shoes that looked too small for her feet. They laced up the side and were always coming untied. She couldn't lean over and tie them, so my mother always offered to have me do it, which made me feel very important. One time she brought me a small bottle of Black Narcissus perfume.

The day of Fancy Work Mother had Mrs. French come early in the morning and make dozens of tiny sandwiches with the crusts cut off, and little cakes individually iced. There was some kind of bright salad made of Jell-O and fruit. Mother made the coffee herself. She put a large kettle of water on the stove, filled a cloth bag with a pound of coffee, put it in the kettle and let it come to a boil, then simmer for a while. The whole house was filled with the aroma of coffee. And on Fancy Work Day we had real cream.

The dining room was quite large and had a sort of sun porch at one end that was actually part of the dining room. Mother got out her Havilland china and the sterling silver and my father bought flowers. On the white linen cloth it looked beautiful.

During the afternoon my sisters entertained for the ladies. Martha played the piano and sang and Lu played her violin. I don't know how good they were. I thought they were wonderful and longed to be old enough to play my violin. Would I ever be good enough?

My father came home from the store just before the ladies were getting ready to leave. He always wore a dark suit, white shirt and tie. Mother insisted that he should go in and make an appearance. My father was quite handsome and the ladies must have thought so too because they all fluttered around him talking and laughing at the same time. He just smiled and nodded and didn't need to say much at all. I think he was glad to get back into the kitchen.

After the ladies left, we were allowed to drink coffee. There never was anything that tasted as wonderful as that coffee with real cream. Perhaps it was the china cup or just the excitement of the ladies of Fancy Work Day.

fragments

My Turn

"Send the children down. Mr. Thurman is here and wants to see the children."

My father was calling Mother from the hardware store. Mr. Thurman was the salesman who had been coming to the store for many years. Each time he came he wanted to see the children.

The time I remember most vividly I was six-years-old, very small for my age. My brother Milt was five, Jimmy four and Charlie almost two. We were all willing to get dressed in our best clothes because the boys had told me that Mr. Thurman weighed them and gave them shiny quarters. The year before I had tonsillitis and didn't get to go.

Milt was determined to have a pompadour so each night he soaked his hair, combed it straight back and wore one of Mother's black stockings over his head. In the morning it was half pompadour and the other half looked like someone had used an egg beater on it. The look on Mother's face warned us not to laugh.

Mother dressed Charlie in a pale green linen suit with a wide white collar, short pants with white buttons down the sides. He wore long white stockings and white shoes. He looked beautiful with his bright blond hair and big blue eyes.

I wore my pink dress with a ribbon to match on top of my head, long white stockings and the most wonderful pair of shoes! The bottoms were black patent leather, the tops white kid, with a tassel on each shoe.

Mother decided we could go by ourselves if we pulled Charlie on the red wagon. It was just a block to the store and she would watch at her end while Mr. Irwin, one of the clerks, would watch for us at the store. She put a fluffy white blanket

60

in the wagon, sat Charlie carefully in, folding the blanket around him.

"Hold on tight, Charlie!" Mother cautioned. And we were off!

The boys went ahead pulling the wagon. I brought up the rear, watching Charlie and admiring my tassels. Charlie squealed with delight at the unexpected outing.

Along the way, Aunt Jane, who spent her life listening in on the party line, put the phone down long enough to call out, "Just like Mary showing off those kids again. Humph, sending them down alone, too." She hurried back to report the news.

Further along, sweet Aunt Mary Warner came down off the porch to give Charlie a hug and kiss. "Going to see your daddy? You all look just lovely in your Sunday clothes."

Before we got there one of Jimmy's pant legs was hanging down around his ankles. Milt's tie was under his ear and his shoe laces were untied. His Alfalfa hair-do was waving in the breeze.

Mr. Irwin helped us into the store, lifted Charlie out of the wagon. Charlie ran on wobbly legs to his dad.

Mr. Thurman exclaimed how nice we all looked and congratulated Dad on his beautiful family. Now was the time we were waiting for. Mr. Thurman walked over to the big scales, took off the bucket that was used to weigh nails, and placed it on the floor. We were ready.

"Who's going to be first?" he asked.

Dad said, "Charlie's the youngest, let's start with him."

Mr. Thurman placed Charlie on the scales while he laughed and squirmed and thought it was a great game. The clerks stood around and laughed and told Charlie he was a darling. Mr. Thurman told him what a nice boy he was and handed him back to Dad. He took a shiny quarter out of his pocket to give to Charlie.

Dad shook his head; "He'll just put it in his mouth."

fragments

Then it was Jimmy's turn to be lifted onto the scales, to be told what a nice big boy he was, how much he'd grown.

"Do you want to grow up to be big like your dad and help in the store?" Jimmy looked Mr. Thurman straight in the eyes and never said a word. Then he was lifted down and Mr. Thurman reached in his pocket and brought out a shiny quarter.

Milt's turn was next, to be told what a nice big boy he was. "Are you going to help your dad in the store?" he asked.

I'm going to be a farmer like my grandpa and ride horses."

"Are you and Jimmy twins?

Milt scoffed at the idea. "I'm in school. Jimmy is a baby."

Then he was lifted down and given a shiny quarter.

Now it is my turn. My heart is pounding so hard I can hear it. My turn to be lifted onto the scales and be told what a nice big girl I am. I go to real school, not kindergarten. He might even think I'm pretty even though I have green eyes and straight hair. I'll smile a lot. My ribbon is on straight, and he'll see my beautiful tasseled shoes. My turn to be lifted onto the scales.

But Mr. Thurman turns, shakes hands with my father and they walk to the front of the store.

I didn't cry. I'm a big girl.

62

fragments

Wood Street School

I couldn't wait to go to Wood Street School. All that summer before I was six we talked about Wood Street, a magic place, a scary place. The day arrived and I went to a beautiful old red brick building. I walked up the wide steps on the girls' side hanging on to the iron railing with one hand, clutching my new blue pencil box and my red tablet with the other.

The boys' side was a few feet away separated by flowers and well-manicured lawn. You didn't dare step on the boys' side or we thought we'd be arrested and carried off to jail.

The boys wore short pants, black shoes and stockings and light colored shirts. They all had short hair and wore peaked caps. They screamed and yelled and pummeled each other and turned cartwheels over the railings.

The girls, in starched dresses, knee socks and sturdy shoes, kept saying in loud voices, "Boys are dumb! Boys are dumb!" All the while looking over to see if the boys were listening.

Finally the bell rings---the signal to get in line and quiet down. When there is complete silence, Daddy Flowers, the janitor, opens the wide doors. The loud music of the Washington Post March fills the air and we march in. The line is straight. We look neither to the right nor left. Mrs. Hartford, our grim-faced principal, stands half way down the hall, ruler in hand.

The older boys have told us about the spanking machine in her office. She straps you in, starts the paddle, and it goes until she thinks you have been punished enough. Just the thought of the paddle machine makes you wish you'd never been born. We don't move an eyeball.

fragments

My room is small, perhaps twenty children, four rows of desks with attached seats. The rows are straight; the desks are bolted to the floor. The floor is made of wood oiled to a dark walnut. We are given books that we arrange in our desks with our fat pencils and red tablets. The smell of chalk, the oiled floor and the new books is exhilarating. School has started.

Mary Suthern was a big girl who sat behind me. She was in first grade last year. I heard my mother say she was over-developed, whatever that meant. She knew all the boys and giggled a lot. She started causing me trouble the second week of school. She leaned over to me and whispered, "I know a bad word! Want to hear it?"

"I don't want to hear it."

"I'm gonna tell you anyway."

"I'm not gonna listen."

"I'm gonna tell you," she whispered in my ear.

"Mary Suthern, what are you whispering about?" Miss Tracy's voice was stern.

"I didn't say nothin."

"Did Mary say something to you?" the teacher stands by my desk.

"She said a bad word!" I start to cry.

"I didn't say nothin," Mary mumbles.

The teacher leans down. "Tell me what she said at once. I'll have none of that bad talk in this room."

I whisper through a torrent of tears, "Underpants!"

One day Mary Suthern asked me if I knew where babies came from. I didn't have a clue. She threatened to tell me. In a way I wanted to know but I was afraid to find out---especially from Mary Suthern.

The previous summer I had visited my cousin Pinkie who was just my age. Uncle Doc made house calls and sometimes he took Pinkie and me along and we stayed in the car. We heard him say he was going to deliver a baby. This was our chance to find out.

"I'll have to get a bite to eat and then I'll be ready," Uncle Doc said.

He always wore a long gray overcoat winter and summer. It had deep pockets, deep enough to carry a baby. While Pinkie kept watch I examined his coat---no baby. I looked in his black bag but found only rows of small bottles and that thing he puts in his ears to listen to your heart.

"We'll wait in the car," Pinkie told her father.

This gave us a chance to examine the car. We didn't find a baby, and Uncle Doc didn't make any stops on the way.

When we arrived at the farmhouse, Uncle Doc said, "Stay in the car now; I won't be long."

Pinkie immediately got out of the car to check the back door. I kept my eyes on the front door. Nobody entered or came out. Pinkie walked around the house, through a cornfield and a vegetable garden and back to the car. No sign of a baby.

So we sat and waited and after a while we heard a baby crying! It was all a mystery.

So you can see why I really wanted to know about babies. But I didn't trust Mary Suthern to tell me the truth.

Day after day she threatened to tell me.

At recess we got in line and marched to the bathroom. We stood outside and were sent in four at a time. I hated the bathroom. It was big and cold and smelled bad. The paper towels were brown and coarse and the floors were always damp and dark.

"I'm gonna tell you today," Mary Suthern said.

fragments

"I don't have to go. I'll just wait in the hall," I said to the teacher.

"You'll go now when I tell you to go. I'm not bringing you down here again."

Miss Tracy sounded cross.

As soon as I got inside, Mary Suthern and her friend Rita pushed me down on the damp floor and sat on me.

"Now don't make a sound or you'll be sorry forever."

Then Mary Suthern whispered in my ear, "Babies grow inside you and when they want to come out the doctor cuts you open down the middle!"

I ran screaming from the bathroom. Miss Tracy called my mother and she came and got me.

Next day I'm back in school. At dismissal time the bell rings and we have five minutes to put books and papers away, to sit up straight and fold our hands on our desks. Another bell and we immediately form two lines and take our partner's hand. I dawdle, hoping to miss my place in line and avoid my partner's hand. A sharp reprimand from Miss Tracy nips that in the bud. My worst fears are realized. I obediently but reluctantly take Billy Pepper's hand. He grins. The Washington Post March begins and we march out. I plan how to escape a fate worse than death. When we get to the end of the school grounds and the line breaks I'll run like the wind. The music stops, the line breaks, I'm too late! Billy Pepper kisses me! Then Billy Pepper sings, "I love coffee, I love tea, I love Wilma and Wilma loves me!"

Then all the kids yell, "Wilma has a boyfriend!"

I hated Billy Pepper!

I was to go to Wood Street School for eight years. I learned to add and subtract, to say my multiplication tables backwards and forwards, to hate story problems. I learned to say all twenty-four auxiliary verbs at the drop of a hat but can see no earthly reason why anyone would want to hear them or even care. I read all the Zane Grey books and thought they were the height of romance. I fell in love with poetry, especially Shelley and Keats. I carried a small black leather notebook with me where I wrote bits of poetry I liked.

I finally found out there was no spanking machine, but I told the new little kids there was. I learned to outrun Billy Pepper, although by 8th grade I thought he was kinda cute. I learned a little more about babies but not a hell of a lot. When I hear the Washington Post March I find myself straightening up, getting ready to march.

So much for education!

fragments

The Grape Story

When there are seven kids in the family there isn't a bedroom for everyone. When I was sixteen and we moved into a big old house on College Avenue I was relegated to a sun porch off one of the upstairs rooms. My cot was uncomfortable but there was an added attraction which more than made up for the lack of comfort.

Living next door in another big old house was a tall, curly haired boy who looked to be about my age. His bedroom was right across from mine. He waved and grinned when he saw me. My sisters and I spent a good deal of time in a dark room giggling and wondering what his name was, and if he was really as cute as he looked.

Before long I was riding to school each morning with Tom. He had an old Ford which he had to crank furiously to get started. But once it got going it was fun to ride so high in the front seat and it sure beat walking two miles to school.

We had fun together, we were never serious about anything, never talked about any future together, never even thought of it. We laughed a lot and kept up a running nonsensical conversation that no one else could understand. Once in a while we went to the movies, not often, we had no money. I was in and out of his house occasionally as he was in mine.

Evidently his mother was worried about us being together so much. She told us repeatedly that we were young and our whole lives were ahead of us. So--what else was new?

One day she said she wanted to talk to me alone. Tom looked rather curious. She took me into another room. I wondered what it was all about but I wasn't in any hurry.

"Have you ever noticed grapes, purple grapes, growing on the vines?" she asked.

"Yes, but I like green ones better."

"I'm talking about purple grapes growing on the vines."

"Oh, yes we have those. We have a grape arbor in the back yard."

"Do you ever pick them?"

"I don't like to, worms drop on you."

"Yes." She said quickly, "but have you seen how delicate and fragile they are?"

"Good pie, too," I said, "but Mom says it's hard to make."

"I'm not talking about what you can make out of them," she said impatiently. "I want you to think about how they look, how luminous and delicate they are, sort of a silvery sheen over each perfect grape. But when they are handled they lose their sheen and become smudged. That luster can never be brought back once they've been handled."

"I guess that's right. I never thought of it."

"Well, I hope you'll remember this story about the grapes."

"Oh, I will; thank you for telling me."

"What did she want?" asked Tom.

"She told me a little story about grapes."

"What for?"

"I don't know. I guess she likes grapes."

One Weekend

When Ben asked me to go to Mentor-on-the-Lake for the weekend, it was just what I needed after the hectic days of exams, proms, and graduation. We would go with Howard in his small car. His girl, Kate, was spending the summer there at her parents' cottage. It was about a five-hour drive. We arrived in time for a cookout on the beach. The food was fabulous, the company entertaining and we were made most welcome.

After dinner Dr. and Mrs. Taylor went back to the cottage. They reminded us to douse the fire, and not to stay up too late. It was a perfect summer night. For a long time we sat in silence. The lapping of the waves, the bright stars and the low embers of the fire were mesmerizing.

"If I were a little taller I'd pick out a star for you," Ben said. "one for you and one for Kate."

I wanted that night to last forever. Everything seemed within reach. Hadn't the speaker at the graduation told us to go out there and accomplish our dreams? The whole world was out there waiting for us, unlimited horizons? We didn't quite believe it, but that night all things seemed possible for tomorrow and tomorrow and all the tomorrows.

"What are you going to do now, Howard?"

"I'll work in Dad's store and take classes at night at the college. Maybe later I can go full time."

"I've been accepted at Ohio Wesleyan," Ben said. "I guess I'll take it easy this summer. Dad and I are training a couple of horses. Then in August we're going to Ireland for a week or two."

"Wow! Ben, how lucky can you get!"

"I'm going to Wellesley where my mother graduated. No boys, I don't know if I can survive." Kate said.

"Thanksgiving will come before you know it," Howard said.

"I suppose you'll be going steady with someone by that time."

"Don't count on it."

"I'm going to the local college," I said. "That is if I can find a part time job. I've signed up for journalism and creative writing. I'm excited about that."

When the fire had dwindled down to a few embers, we doused it and covered it with sand.

"I'll race you to the cottage!" Kate said.

Mrs. Taylor had arranged our sleeping quarters. Kate and I upstairs, the boys downstairs on the sleeping porch. At midnight we all wandered into the kitchen for a snack. We stood around the table eating cheese and crackers and drinking milk.

I was wearing a bright blue coolie coat, a short sort of Chinese coat with a belt over white cotton pajamas, and bare feet. Kate looked glamorous in a pink robe all lace and ribbons and slippers to match. Howard had on J.C. Penney's best blue and white striped cotton pajamas. Ben wore dark red silk pajamas and soft beige leather slippers.

Ben took a banana from a basket of fruit on the table. He stood there, his blond hair over his forehead, looking funny and awfully young. He was trying to peel his banana.

Finally Howard said, "Ben, you're peeling it at the wrong end!"

That seemed terribly funny and we laughed until Mrs. Taylor came out and said we'd better be off to bed because tomorrow would be a big day.

After breakfast we got into bathing suits and were off to the beach. I wore my bright green two-piece bathing suit that

71

I thought was quite dashing. Kate was all in white. We took a blanket along to lie on the beach and soak up some sun.

Our stretch of beach was almost deserted. A perfect day, just enough sun, just enough breeze. Ben and I lay on our blanket inches apart, never touching, just smiling into each other's eyes. Several times we went for a swim. Once we waded waist-deep out to a small island and sat there pretending we were marooned. We took long walks up the shore and picked out the cottages we liked, what we'd do to improve others. Then back to lie on the beach.

At dusk there was another picnic. I remember we had corn done on the grill, steaks, finger salad and fresh strawberries. It was a perfect day.

We had to leave Sunday evening. Kate was to stay another two weeks and Howard had to get back to work. We tried to get an early start but Kate was reluctant to leave Howard so we didn't get started until nine o'clock. We weren't in the car half an hour until Ben was sound asleep. I sat in the middle, a small car with no back seat. Ben kept falling over on me. I finally just left his head on my shoulder.

"Give him a push," Howard said. "He doesn't need to lean on you."

"He's okay. He's sleeping so soundly I hate to bother him."

"Talk to me, or I'm afraid I'll go to sleep too!"

"What do you want to talk about?"

"Anything, just talk."

"Do you think zebras are white with black stripes or black with white stripes?"

"I think they're white with black stripes."

"But do you really know? Have you examined a zebra carefully?"

"No,, but I'll settle for white with black stripes."

"Did you ever know a zebra personally?"

"Aren't they all alike?"

"Not to another zebra."
We were silent for awhile just watching the long black ribbon of road unwind.
"Are you in love with Ben?"
"I haven't decided."
"He's in love with you."
"I know."
"Are you in love with Kate?"
"I haven't decided."
"She's in love with you."
"I know."
"We're a couple of mugwumps."
"Give Ben a push."
"He's fine, don't worry about it."
"Do you think a person can get into another time zone?" I ask.
"What do you mean? Like suddenly living in 1600 maybe?'
"Yes, wouldn't that be fun?"
"Yeah, but it couldn't happen."
"Maybe all time starts at the same place, like trains all starting at the same station, one 1600, one 1700, and so forth up to the present time. But maybe an avalanche, or a terrible accident, or an earthquake and you are suddenly plummeted into another zone."
"Plummeted! What's plummeted?"
"You know, suddenly thrown violently."
"Sounds unlikely but interesting. Could you ever get back?"
"Maybe, but what if you didn't want to?"
"I would! But would I know about now?
"But you would try and get back?" I asked.
"Plummeted you mean?"
"Yeah, plummeted."
"I'm not going to be plummeted, I hate that word."
"You have to be plummeted."
"Not me!"

fragments

"Then you'll just have to stay there forever!"
Silence for awhile as we think about that.
I look over at Howard. In alarm, I say, "Are zebras white with..."
"I'm awake, I'm awake!"
"Do you believe in dreams?" I ask.
"I don't think they mean anything but I dream quite often."
"What about?"
"Things all jumbled up, but other times about the family or work. What about you?"
"I dream about people I've never seen or read about. I can see them just as plainly as if I were there. I can see the house, the rooms, the furniture. So do you ever do that?"
"Can't say that I do. What do you think is the answer?"
"I think I've gotten into someone else's dream. Some way dreams have been crossed and I'm in another person's dream."
"You're crazy, you know that!"
"Crazy nice, or crazy crazy?"
"I'll reserve my opinion."
"I won't talk anymore then."
After a bit Howard says, "You do like Ben, don't you?"
"What's not to like? He's a real dreamboat, he's smart and he's rich!"
"He doesn't know how to peel a banana."
"There's that!"
We're three-quarters of the way home. Howard's head is nodding.
"Let's sing, that'll keep you awake."
We sing One Blue Bottle Hanging' on the Wall, Two Blue Bottles Hangin' on the Wall all the way up to fifty and back down. Then a little bit of Old Mc Donald. Howard makes all the animal sounds.
"You can't sing very well," Howard says.

74

"I know. The music teacher told me I had perfect pitch but a range of only six notes."

"That's bad, six notes."

"Yeah but perfect pitch!"

"Do you like music?" I ask.

"Tommy Dorsey, Glenn Miller, all the big bands. I go for them. What about you?"

"I like the big bands for dancing, you know that. But for listening, I prefer classical music. But sometimes, sometimes it's too much."

"What do you mean too much?"

"Are you familiar with Rachmaninoff's Rhapsody on a Theme by Paganini? It's my favorite music in all the world. But sometimes all that magnificently passionate music soaring into the sky makes me feel like I'll shatter into a million pieces. I have to turn it off."

Howard pats my knee.

"Do we have anything to eat in this car?"

"I have a Clark Bar I'll share."

"We're almost home, want to waken Ben?"

I try but Ben just mumbles.

"Poor old Ben, He's dead to the world."

So here we are. Howard pulls up in front of my house. I move Ben carefully so that his head rests on the back of the seat. I kiss him lightly and whisper, "Thank you for a super weekend!"

Howard walks me to the door. "I'll get Ben home safe and sound," he says. He takes my hand, kisses me lightly on the cheek. "I hope we can discuss zebras another time."

fragments

Isaly's

During my freshman year in college in a small town in Pennsylvania, I applied for a job at an Isaly store. My duties were to make cones and sundaes and wait on a few customers. My hours were from three until closing which was shortly after nine.

When I got there my first day the boss told me to go to the kitchen and wash dishes. I expected a few glasses or ice cream bowls. Instead every available space was literally filled with dishes and utensils, pots and pans and dirty paper napkins. But I started! No electric dishwasher, just a very deep sink, hot water and soap. I would wash as many as I could get on the counter, dry them and start over on a new batch.

At nine-o'clock my father came to get me, thinking I'd need a ride home after my first day at work. When the manager told him I was in the kitchen and he learned that I had been washing dishes without a break for six hours he was furious. He made me quit immediately.

I told the boss I was quitting and he refused to pay me because I hadn't worked there long enough.

For awhile we all stayed away from Isaly's. But they did have the very best ice cream and my father said the boss probably didn't realize I had been in the kitchen that long, and anyway, we might as well forget it. So we started going back once in a while.

When the family all got together, my three sisters, three brothers, Mother, Dad, my grandmother and my best friend Bertie, we decided to walk to Isaly's for ice cream. Dad was in high good humor, told us to order whatever we wanted.

We pushed several tables together, sat down talking and laughing and deciding what to order. We decided on Banana

Splits, Carmel Marshmallow Nut Sundaes with Chocolate Ice Cream, sodas, milkshakes. The choices were unbelievable! We had a super marvelous time!

When it was almost closing time the waitress brought the bill. The manager was at the cash register. Dad said he'd go first, we all followed.

Dad handed the bill to the manager and said, "I think this takes care of the money you owe my daughter." We all filed out, suppressing our laughter, until we got outside.

The Statehouse Inn

The first time I saw Nashville, Tennessee, I thought it an enchanted place. I went there to visit my sister, Lu, whose husband Lloyd was a medical student at Vanderbilt. I was so enthralled I decided to stay. They had rented a large house, and to make enough money for Lloyd to stay in med school, they rented rooms to three other medical students.

We all had dinner together in the evening. Lu was an excellent cook, and the fellows liked staying there. At mealtime the conversation was all about patients, operations, childbirth, autopsies and cadavers. They laughed uproariously at the most sad and outrageous situations. I was so shocked I could scarcely eat. I came from a very conservative family where subjects such as those were never mentioned, especially at the dinner table. But after a while I came to realize that the fellows were almost as shocked as I was. What with very little sleep, long hours at the hospital, worry over exams and money, they were simply letting off steam.

To stay in Nashville I had to get a job. After a few weeks, I was working as a waitress at the State House Inn. It was an exclusive restaurant, just a few blocks from the State House. I had absolutely no experience, but I think I got the job because I was from the North and the owners who had never been out of Tennessee, thought people would be amused by the funny way I talked.

The owners, Anna and Glenn, brother and sister, had inherited the restaurant from their father. They were very good-looking and had excellent taste in clothes. They worked very hard in the kitchen, but the minute they entered the dining room they had the beautiful manners and warmth of the Old South. The restaurant was very successful.

fragments

There was one other waitress, Betty. She had never been anywhere except back and forth to work and a date every night with her boyfriend. She was happy to work, live at home and save her money to get married. We got along but I really never got to know her even after working with her for almost a year.

Tillie was the cook. She was tiny, weighed about ninety pounds, and was very black. Glenn told me Tillie had nine children, no husband, and kept them all together by working at the restaurant. The kitchen was her own domain and no one dared step a foot inside. She was usually in a good humor giggling and talking to Glenn, but sometimes she got furious, and then we all kept out of her way until she calmed down.

John Henry washed dishes. He was tall and dark and quite handsome. All day long he stood beside that deep sink, his arms in soapy water up to his elbows, washing dishes, spraying them and stacking them in huge wire racks. He mumbled all the time he worked.

I confess that I had never met a black person and was particularly interested in both John Henry and Tillie. They definitely didn't share my interest. They treated me quite coolly, never rude, just indifferent. Tillie never spoke to me directly except one morning to say, "Are you Jewish?" When I said I wasn't, there was no reaction one way or the other. I think she was suspicious of anyone from the North.

My hours were long, the pay quite meager. I worked a split shift, started at eight, and worked until one, off until five, and back until nine or whenever the last customer left. There wasn't enough time in the afternoon to go home, and not enough money to ride the streetcar anyway, so I spent the time exploring the city. If I got tired of that, I sat in a hotel lobby until they told me to move; then I'd find another. I got to know all the hotel lobbies in downtown Nashville. In spite of everything, I found Southern life to be quite exciting.

fragments

The kitchen was long and low, a comforting sort of place. Here I was permitted to have my evening meal so I no longer ate at my sister's. Tillie cooked four vegetables every day, never the same four. I could have all the vegetables I wanted and cornbread and grits, never any meat, never any dessert, never biscuits for which Tillie was famous. There was always coffee with cream. Tillie could do magic things with vegetables---black-eyed peas, turnip greens, okra, cabbage, sweet potatoes, Swiss chard, squash, kale, always cooked to perfection. At first being a rather persnickety eater I chose one vegetable, but it wasn't long until I was eating four every day. I didn't eat breakfast, because no one ever said I could, so I just drank coffee. I did notice that every morning Tillie cooked ham and eggs and biscuits for Betty.

One day I asked Glenn, "Why is John Henry always muttering?"

"He's the preacher on Sunday at his church and he's trying to learn the 23rd Psalm."

"Why doesn't he bring the book along?"

"He can't read. He hears it from someone else and tries to remember it."

As I went about my work from kitchen to dining room I'd hear him saying "He leadeth me beside the still waters, He restoreth my soul, He restoreth my soul, He restoreth my soul."

It drove me crazy! I wanted him to get on with it. It was like a child learning to play the piano and getting stuck. Out of desperation I said, "He leadeth me in the paths of righteousness for His name's sake."

A few weeks later he was repeating over and over and over, "Yeah though I walk through the valley of the shadow of death, I will fear no evil, I will fear no evil, I will fear no evil."

And I supplied, "For Thou art with me, Thy rod and Thy staff they comfort me."

This went on for months. John Henry never said a word but he kept learning the psalm as I supplied the lines.

Then one morning Tillie said, "I fixed your breakfast, Miss Billie." She placed a plate of ham and eggs and biscuits in front of me. I wondered what had happened but was so pleased and surprised that I didn't question anything. When I finished eating, Tillie said, "Miss Billie, John Henry has a surprise for you."

John Henry took his hands out of the deep soapy water, dried them carefully on a long white towel, removed his big blue apron and turned around facing me. He stood proud and tall his faced wreathed in smiles. Then getting serious, his good black face alight with love, he repeated those beautiful age-old words right down to the very end. "Surely goodness and mercy shall follow me all the days of my life and I shall dwell in the house of the Lord forever."

fragments

Local Color

I arrived in Boston at the age of twenty, excited about exploring a new place. I had lived in Nashville while my sister's husband was a medical student at Vanderbilt, now he was interning at Long Island Hospital in Boston Harbor. I couldn't miss an opportunity to see a different part of the country.

My sister lived on Beacon Hill in one of those old four-story mansions that had been made into six small apartments, two on each floor. At that time Beacon Hill was a mixture of the very rich and the very poor. One house made into apartments would be right next to a mansion still occupied by the original family living in luxury.

We lived in Apartment #3. The El roared past every few minutes seeming to shake the whole building, cups and saucers rattled and the lights dimmed.

In the center of the house there was a chute which went up to all four floors. Originally this had been a dumb waiter that carried food up from the kitchen basement. Now the shelves had been removed and small doors left to open on each floor. Day or night we could open the little door and hear everything that was going on in the other five apartments. It was like turning on a radio talk show. We never actually met any of these people but knew more about them than we really needed to know. Of course, opening the door was an option, but we became addicted.

An older couple lived in Apartment #1. They wouldn't climb stairs. They often complained about someone called Horace who drank too much. They were trying to persuade him to go to A.A.

fragments

Apartment #2 had a young child, Ishmael, who was taken to his grandmother's every day while his parents both worked at a restaurant. They always argued, in a mixture of Italian and broken English, about whose turn it was to pick him up.

Apartment #4 was a woman of indeterminate age who had lots and lots of company, mostly men. At that time I wasn't aware of her job.

Apartment #5 was seldom at home except for a quick meal.

The newlyweds occupied apartment #6. Morning, noon or night they were in a state of ecstasy.

I decided I'd like to stay in Boston if I could find a job. I finally landed one in a Nu-Enamel store in Cambridge. I decided to get a place near the store, although I knew I'd miss that crazy weird apartment on Beacon Hill. I found a boarding house with Annie Ware. She made me feel welcome the minute she saw me. She was little and thin with white hair and merry blue eyes, always anticipating something new and exciting.

There were five other boarders, all men. I had a room on the third floor, a room thirty feet long furnished beautifully, my breakfast each morning and dinner at night---all for seven dollars a week!

I'll have to admit that I soon became the darling of the boarding house, probably because I was thirty years younger than any of them. They were interested in my dates, always wanted to be introduced, wanted to hear about my job and admired my clothes. I did little errands for them, like picking up aspirin at the drug store or leaving something at the dry cleaners. From my boarding house I could easily walk to my job at the Nu-Enamel store.

My job description was to wait on customers, to sell paint and wallpaper. I could do that, piece of cake! After a couple of weeks something new was added. I had to stand in the big window at the front of the store and paint.

fragments

I would paint a small table or chair in a bright color, paint a few strokes then point to a sign "One Coat Covers," paint a few more strokes and point to another sign "No Brush Marks," to another "Easy To Apply," to another "Comes In All Colors, Colors Won't Fade." I painted and pointed, painted and pointed, until the chair or table was completely painted. I was told to look up and smile between paintings. I wrote and told my mother about my new job and she immediately made several smocks for me to wear in the window.

One Saturday, I was in the window wearing a yummy pink smock. The store was just a few blocks from Harvard. The Harvard boys were out for a good time. I soon realized that quite a crowd was gathering in front of the window. Then the fellows began holding up their own signs: "When Are You Off?" "Do You Have A Boyfriend?" "How Old Are You?" "I'm Available!"

Suddenly the front door opens with a BANG! A policeman screams, "Get that girl out of the window. I have traffic blocked up for a mile!"

On Saturday nights after that I sold wallpaper.

fragments

The Dance

When someone travels 600 miles for a date, it's a reason for some sort of celebration. Bill had come from Ohio to Boston where I had come to visit my sister and then decided to get a job and stay for awhile.

We were walking down the mid-way at Revere Beach looking for a place to dance. I was wearing a delectable blue dress and white sandals, and Bill looked quite dashing in a blue sports coat and white slacks. The midway was a place of happy chaos. Little kids were begging for another ride on the merry-go-round, teen-agers were jostling to get in line for the roller coaster, couples were getting out of boats that made trips through underground waterways, the girls looking disheveled, the boys embarrassed.

Hucksters were trying to outdo each other.

"Get weighed over here! Come on, Little Lady. If I can't guess your weight you get a prize. Don't be bashful! Who's gonna be next?"

"Shoot the ducks! Come on, fellas, win a kewpie doll for your sweetie!"

"Get a picture with your girl! Two bits and she'll never forget you!"

It was all noise and fake and glitter and we loved it! But it wasn't quite what we were looking for. We passed the hotdog stand, the cotton candy, the french fries, the taffy that glistened like satin as it was pulled on huge machines. We walked on beyond the crowd where the park was quiet, where flowers bloomed and trees made shade and there were benches where we could relax and feel the quiet.

Then we heard music. It was coming from a wide white building, the veranda a mass of flowers and ferns. "That's

85

our song, *Moon-glow!* Let's go!"

Bill pulled me unresisting into the building. We looked around for a place to buy a ticket, not seeing one we simply started to dance.

There's something about moving onto a polished dance floor that is unlike anything else. Your partner holds you lightly, the air is awash with music and joy and rhythm.

When the piece ended and the band went into *Did You Ever See a Dream Walking* and Bill whispered that he did, I fell tentatively in love.

Then suddenly I was dancing with a tall guy wearing a red bow tie and a bright smile. It seemed a little strange but he was quite nice and very polite.

"Where are you from?" he asked.

"Ohio."

"Oh, you're from out West."

"Ohio," I repeated, thinking he hadn't heard me.

"I never met a girl from the West before. I'd like to go there some time. Are all the little girls out West as pretty as you?"

"No, I'm one of the plainer ones."

I got a glimpse of Bill dancing with a tall redhead. I looked at him questionably; he shrugged his shoulders.

Red Bow Tie thanked me and I was immediately dancing with a short chubby fellow.

"Hi, Ohio, this must be my dance." News gets around fast I thought. He danced around the room like a whirling dervish. Fun but rather exhausting.

Back with Bill again. "Hey, this Boston! It's got to be the friendliest place I've ever been in."

"Yeah, imagine this at a public dance at home!"

My next partner was a little guy about my size. He pushed me around the room like a vacuum cleaner and talked all the time.

"Ride horses?" he asked.

"Yes, sometimes." I laughed as I remembered old sway-backed Saidie that Grandfather brought into the yard and all six of us kids got on her back as she plodded patiently around the pasture.

My next partner was a dark fellow with thick glasses who looked as if he had been sitting over bank ledgers forever.

"Howdy, Pardner!" he said.

"Howdy, yourself!" If he wanted West, I'd go along.

He was such a superb dancer that I changed my mind about his occupation and decided he must be a dance instructor. He wanted to know all about the West but he talked so much that I really didn't need to say anything and it's a good thing because at that time I had never been west of Chicago.

Once in a while I'd get a chance to dance with Bill. "Did you buy a ticket?"

"No, I guess you buy it at the end of the dance."

A real dreamboat cut in as the band started to play *Day is Done*. I swear to you we never moved more than ten inches during the entire piece. It was actually hugging to music. I rather liked it, a hug now and then can't hurt.

After that a fat jolly man in a plaid blazer walked me around the room and back to the starting place. He couldn't have cared if they were playing *Sweet Gerogia Brown* or *Stars and Stripes Forever*.

I think I must have danced with every man in the place. In between all these characters I did get to dance with Bill.

At midnight Red Bow Tie rang a bell and everyone cheered. He announced that it was time for refreshments. Double doors were pushed open to reveal a beautiful dining room. It was a banquet! The long table was set with sterling silver, white linen cloth and flowers everywhere. There was a chef at one end slicing succulent pieces of roast beef. There was shrimp, lobster and crab. All sorts of relishes, fruit, hot rolls, muffins and bread sticks. There were cakes and dozens of delicate cookies.

I looked at Bill in alarm, "Enough money?" I whispered.

"Yes," he nodded. He looked overcome. "But maybe we'd better get out of here."

Before we could move, Red Bow Tie grabbed my hand and said, "You two can sit with me. I reserved your places."

"You've done it again, Phil!"

So Red Bow Tie was Phil. He stood up, tapped the glass for silence. "Our caterer has once again lived up to his famous reputation. But before we begin to enjoy this wonderful food I want to thank Paul for bringing his delightful guests."

"I'd like to take credit but they are Kenny's guests."

"Sorry, I didn't bring them, wish I had. They came with Brad and Betty."

Bill was sputtering. He said in a croaking voice, "We aren't anybody's guests."

I was shrinking down in my chair wondering if I could possibly get under the table and away. "We just came in and started to dance," I said in a weak voice.

"You mean you crashed this party?" Phil said in amazement.

"We'll leave, we apologize, we're sorry!" Bill started to get up from the table. Phil put his hand on Bill's shoulder and pushed him down. We waited to be thrown out, or whatever they do in Boston when they apprehend crooks.

Phil continued. "This is a very exclusive club, one of the most exclusive clubs in Boston. No one has ever, I mean ever, crashed one of our parties. We have two a year, one at Christmas at our club, one here in the summer. People would sell their grandmothers for an invitation to one of our parties."

He very slowly looked around the table at each guest. Complete silence. Then I heard a small giggle, then another. Then a burst of laughter rippled around the whole table.

88

"Sit down and enjoy!" someone yelled. And we did!

Finally the band begins to play *Goodnight Sweetheart*. It's the last dance. Everyone dances with his own partner.

It's time for us to leave.

"Goodbye, Ohio!"

"Good luck, Ohio!"

"Say a good word for us out West!"

"Crash our party anytime, Ohio!"

"Good luck, good luck, good luck!"

Perhaps somewhere in Boston two old people are reminiscing. "Remember that dance we had when that young couple from out West crashed our party?"

"I remember. I danced with that tall young fellow. How he could dance!"

"I danced with that pretty little girl. Best party we ever had!" He sits silent for a minute. "Wonder where they are now?"

Regina

"We're invited to a party at Regina's. Do you want to go?" asked Matt. "I think you'll have fun, but we can leave if you get bored. Regina's parties are something else!"

"What time?"

"Oh anytime between four and whenever, it won't matter."

I had arrived in Phoenix the day before to visit my grandson Matt. I had met Regina a few times briefly when she visited in Ohio. She was a special friend of Matt's and of my granddaughter, Andrea.

Regina works very hard. She works for the Foundation for Senior Living funded by the state of Arizona. The houses are in the valley and each house has six clients. It is less expensive for the state than to keep these people institutionalized. Some of the women have been in mental hospitals for ten or twenty years. They have no friends, no family. Regina is in charge. She has two or three helpers and another nurse comes in to give medication when it is needed. The women have no idea what is going on in the world and have seldom if ever been anywhere. Regina has a van and she takes them to the mall or to the top of the mountain to watch the sunset. She can easily pick up a woman in her strong young arms and help her into the van. They love her because for the first time someone cares. Maybe that is why we are all so fond of Regina.

On weekends Regina relaxes. She turns on the bright lights outside her house and people come. Sometimes friends make a small band and everyone dances. Sometimes no one comes. This doesn't bother Regina.

As we approached the house there was a soft breeze redolent with the scent of lemons, lemons hanging on the trees, lemons covering the ground. The front of the house was strung with lights.

We entered, without knocking, into a large room furnished with two unmatched upholstered chairs piled high with books. Several glowing candles were on a small table.

"When Regina moved here a few years ago there was wall to wall carpet in all the rooms, "Matt said. "Regina didn't like it so she ripped it all up and found these beautiful polished cement floors." They were very unusual, beautiful dark gray. They looked like ceramic tile.

We went through onto a terrace that was the length of the house. Along one side were two large palm trees and a mulberry tree. On the opposite side was a pecan tree. Evening sunlight slanting through the trees turned the flagstone to soft pink.

A large teepee stood beside the mulberry tree. Inside Regina had built a brick oven where she heated stones, poured water over them and sat in the steam to meditate and cleanse her body and soul—an ancient Native American sauna. I thought I'd come back another day and try it.

Regina was over by the grill, grilling chicken and shrimp. Regina is a big handsome woman almost six feet tall with strong brown legs. She was wearing cutoff shorts and a loose yellow shirt. She had pulled her dark hair up on top of her head in a topknot and tied it with a string. When she speaks it is unbelievable. She has the softest loveliest voice I have ever heard!

The music was piped in. A few people were dancing alone, others with partners. There were several deck chairs, a small empty table, no plates, and no napkins. We just sort of sauntered or danced over to the grill and took a piece of chicken or stood there and ate shrimp.

Regina spread her arms wide and said in that amazingly beautiful voice, "Oh, all this wonderful food!"

Regina had placed torches at random around the patio. At one time a torch fell over and started a grass fire. Regina wasn't alarmed. She just danced over in time to the music and stomped it out.

Beyond the pecan tree a twenty-foot hedge hid the neighbor's house. Every few minutes a head appeared above the hedge for an instant. It was quite astonishing until we realized they had a trampoline.

Regina has a big old shaggy dog, part German shepherd and part collie. She named her Thelma. A small cat of the same reddish color follows Thelma around. Regina calls her Thelma Jr. Five other cats of unknown origin wander aimlessly around the palm trees. They are Serengeti, Casey Jones, Opie Taylor, Cassidy and Fraidy Cat.

Gaby was from California from a very wealthy family. She was a free spirit, didn't like all that money. Regina was getting ready to go to Belize for a vacation. Just off hand Gaby said she'd like to go along. Regina thought that would be fun so Gaby quit her job and was getting ready to go. After Belize Gaby was going to Spain.

Gaby reminded us so much of Ellen DeGeneres of TV fame that we all started calling her Ellen. She went right along with it and acted as much like Ellen as Ellen herself. She kept it up all evening and was the life of the party.

About twenty people wandered in. Valerie was a quiet girl, as tall as Regina. She wore baggy dark green pants and a long purple shirt. She never quit dancing by herself, languidly, almost in slow motion – over to the grill and back, always smiling. Once when the music had a good fast beat she grabbed a man near her and danced furiously for a few minutes. When the music ended she went back to dancing alone, dreamily, almost in place.

A trip to the bathroom was an amusing experience. Regina had given two four-year-old kids different colored inkpads and a few rubber stamps and told them to go ahead and do the walls. As far as they could reach were birds, flowers, numbers, addresses every which way. It was more interesting than a book.

By the time we left, the full moon was a golden globe shining through the pecan tree, the torches were making weird streaks of light, soft music was still playing; the guests were still dancing. It seemed unreal. I wondered if I'd wake up tomorrow and find it was all a dream.

My Mother

My mother met my father at an Epworth League party when she was sixteen. He asked to walk her home. And the rest of her life was changed forever. That fall she started to teach school in a one-room schoolhouse, grades one through eight. In the summers she went to Mt. Union College until she graduated. She married my father when she was twenty-three.

Many years later, after my parents were gone, I went through their things and found a bundle of yellow letters tied with a frayed white ribbon, all letters my mother had written to my father while she was apart from him. They were rather formal little letters telling about her pupils, her friends or her classes. They all started "Dearest" and ended "Yours, Mary." They would hardly seem like love letters now, but I'm sure they were.

Mother was lovely. She had beautiful eyes and long dark hair which she wore in kind of an elaborate bun at the back of her head, sometimes with a bright comb, but other times just carelessly pinned up. Her hair was just curly enough that a few wisps always fell down on her forehead. She never wore any make-up, and she could be ready to go anyplace at the drop of a hat.

My Aunt Olive, who was a few years younger than Mother, was always taking courses in "How to Apply Make-up" or enrolling in "Charm School." Dad said Mother had more charm in her little finger than the whole charm school put together. Of course Dad may have been a bit prejudiced. Mother was never a thin person. My father preferred pleasingly plump over thin. Whenever we went home looking,

94

we felt, quite thin and svelte, Dad would say, "You'd better stay home a few weeks and we'll fatten you up."

When I was very small we lived in a large house where four bedrooms opened off of an upstairs hallway. Mother would place a chair in the center and read *Hiawatha* until all six of us fell asleep. Sometimes I'd wake up much later and hear her playing the piano—soft classical music that she loved.

Later when three of us were in college at the same time, tuition had been paid but we still needed books. At the same time, the electric light bill was due and there wasn't enough money for both. Mother didn't hesitate a minute. We bought the books. For the next month we used candles. One night my older sister brought a beau home for dinner. He thought we were the most romantic family he'd ever heard of, to eat by candlelight. Mother believed education was most important. She said the only security we'd ever have was in our heads.

Some one was always bringing home an extra person for dinner, it wasn't unusual to have twelve at the table. If Mother knew it ahead, she'd put in an extra potato or water the stew. One day I said, "Do you think we'll have enough?"

She answered, "Eat it and quit!" That has become a stock saying in our family, "Eat it and quit."

My sisters and I decided we just had to have an evening wrap. My mother had a long black velvet coat that she had had packed away forever. She unearthed it, ripped it and steamed it; we bought a pattern of a short coat with intricate full sleeves. She worked at it a little at a time. But I thought I had to have it the next day, so I decided to go ahead without her and finish it. She told me to wait because she was busy. I was impatient and went ahead with it and botched it! I ran to her for help. She took one look at it, threw it down and said, "It's your own fault! Now get out here and help with dinner!" I went to bed that night feeling very sorry for myself. When I got up in the morning there hung my coat, pale pink lining, silver buttons. I knew Mother had sat up half the night finishing my coat. We called it the "Heinz 57 Coat" because of all of the fabric piecing mother had to do. My sisters and I wore it and fought over it for years.

My mother never threw anything away, if she could possibly fix it, make it over, let it out, take it in, dye it, bleach it, trim it, shorten it or lengthen it.

Mother had great powers of persuasion. One day she saw a truck in front of the house that was coming from an excavation. It was carrying a huge rock, actually a boulder, about five feet wide and four feet high. She had always wanted just such a rock for the backyard. The children could play King of the Mountain, Cowboys and Indians, and all sorts of fun games on that rock. She hurried out and explained to the men on the truck just why she needed the rock. They unloaded it exactly where she wanted it. For years it was the favorite place for the grandchildren.

She used to come to visit me here in Huron. When Dad was busy she would ride the bus from Alliance. The bus stopped in Huron and Sandusky – no stops in between. She simply explained to the bus driver about her little granddaughter, and the new baby she hadn't yet seen, showed him pictures, and smiled, so he said he guessed he could make an exception. He let her off right at the end of Cincinnati Avenue, helped her off with her luggage and waved good-bye.

I can see her now, coming down the road, carrying her white suitcase, wearing a beautiful suit, possibly light gray or soft pink and always a hat, she loved hats. It was a dirt road then, forest on both sides. The sunlight filtered down through the branches and the road sloped down to the blue waters of the lake. We'd be sitting in front of the house watching for her.

Sometimes when I'm cooking, using an old recipe of Mother's which calls for "…a little of this and a little of that," and "two eggs if they're cheap," and I'm not sure just what

fragments

she meant, I momentarily think, I'll call Mother, she'll know,
and realize with a pang and a sharp sense of grief that she is
no longer here. But as long as I'm alive on this earth, part of
me will be my mother.

fragments

The Garage Door

I press the button for the garage door. It shrieks and grumbles, gets started, then comes to a slow grumbling halt. Abruptly it continues with a sad wheeze and continues to the top. My garage door has apnea, some day it will die and fall on me and my old Buick and that will be the end of that.

I want a new garage door, that's all, just a new door, come in the morning, hang the door, cart the old one away – finished. Shouldn't take long, just a few hours, come in the morning, be gone by noon. No fuss, no bother!

I call the garage door man, he'll come the next morning at 8:00, should be finished by noon. He arrives on time.

"Garage doors, that's my business, all I know is garage doors," says the garage door man. After about an hour he calls from the garage. "This telephone wire around the door frame has to be moved, don't know anything about telephone wires. Garage doors are my business."

I call the telephone company, the telephone man arrives shortly. "This never should have been done this way. I didn't do it but I'll re-route it for you," says the telephone man. "By the way, those two wires should be grounded. Who left then that way?"

Maybe the air condition man left them," I say. I call the air condition man. It's a slow day and he comes right over.

"I didn't leave any wires ungrounded. Maybe it was the electrician. I don't know why I'm here. I didn't do anything wrong," says the air condition man.

I call the electrician who comes in about half an hour. "What's this about wires that are ungrounded? It's nothing I did," says the electrician. He notices that the wires above the

98

fuse box are not enclosed. "I'll fix those wires. I didn't leave them like that, order must have been lost," says the electrician.

"Garage doors, that's my business, all I know is garage doors," says the garage door man.

"Those must have been left by the cable man," says the electrician.

"I don't why I'm here, I didn't do anything wrong," says the air condition man.

I call the cable man. He promises to stop by.

As I go past the downstairs bathroom, I see with alarm that the sink is leaking, the floor is flooded with water. I call the plumber.

The cable man arrives. "I must have left those wires ungrounded," says the cable man.

I don't know why I'm here, I didn't do anything wrong," says the air condition man.

"What's this got to do with garage doors?" asks the cable man.

"It's a long story!" I say.

"Garage doors, all I know is garage doors," says the garage door man.

The plumber arrives. "It's not a big job, have it fixed in a jiffy," says the plumber.

Meanwhile everyone congregates in the garage, watching the garage door man. I don't know what the great fascination is about the garage door.

"Garage doors, been doing it all my life, that's my business, garage doors," says the garage door man.

"Yeah ! Yeah!"

"Sink's as good as new," says the plumber.

"Wires are taken care of, but it wasn't my fault," says the electrician.

"Wires are grounded," says the cable man.

"Telephone wires never should have been through the doorway but I didn't do it," says the telephone man.

"I don't know why I'm here, I didn't do anything wrong," says the air condition man.

"Garage doors, all I know is garage doors," says the garage door man. "And I'm just about finished."

It's the middle of the afternoon and I'm exhausted. The garage door is in place, the old one has been carted away. I think it calls for a celebration. I go to the kitchen and bring out six cans of beer and an ice tea for myself.

"A toast!" says the air condition man. We raise our cans in the air. "Here's to Free Enterprise!"

We drink to that.

"Here's to Public Utilities!" says the telephone man.

We drink to that.

And then the garage door man presses that little white button and that garage door goes up just as smooth as silk!

fragments

Jacob

Five-year-old Jacob came over to spend the afternoon. "I need time away from Hannah," he said. "She's only four, you know."

He was wearing khaki shorts, heavy brown shoes and a tan shirt with a picture of the world and the slogan, "Save the Earth."

What's that on your shirt?" I asked.

"It says save the earth, I can do that."

"You can?"

"Yes, I pick up trash and I put cans in the blue box and I take care of my animals."

"How are your animals?"

"Well, my gecko dried up and I put my turtle outside in the wading pool because I thought he'd like it but the raccoon bit his head off."

"That's terrible!"

"Dad said that's the nature of raccoons, but it didn't help the turtle much."

"My fish are happy," he continued. "They just eat and swim back and forth and look at the shells I put in there."

"That should take care of your fish."

"My cats are OK. Snowflake and Calico Jack are pretty good, but Tripod is wild. Dad says that is because he has only three legs and had to learn to be tough and fight."

I knew he wanted to tell me something else. Finally he said, "Hannah drank black coffee for breakfast. I told her she'd stay little and never get big like you. I told her over and over that she'd just stay little all her life. She wouldn't listen, just kept laughing and drinking her coffee until it was all gone. I told her she'd just have to suffer the con-se-quences."

101

He thought for a minute, then said, "What is that?"

"What's what?"

"The con-se-quences."

"Umm, the result of something."

"Like getting old?"

"No, that's something else. You can't help that. "It's if you do something and there's a certain result."

He looked puzzled, then said, "Like if I jump on the bed and fall off and get hurt I suffer those?"

"You've got it!"

"I guess I'll go and climb a few trees now," he said. And off he went out the front door and into the yard.

After a bit he was back. "I have a good idea," he said. "Let's have a picnic."

"I don't think I have any picnic food."

"I'll check it out," he said cheerfully.

I heard him rummaging around in the kitchen.

"I'll tell you when the picnic is ready. You stay in there and it will be a surprise."

In a short while he was back. "The picnic is ready; it's time to eat."

"Whose picnic is this?" I asked.

"Jacob's."

"Jacob? Who's Jacob?"

"You know, Jacob Andrew Figgins!"

"Oh, that Jacob!"

I take his small warm hand and we walk outside.

"Are we sitting at the picnic table?"

"No, that's just eating outside. This is a *real* picnic."

In the far corner the yard under the pine tree and the corkscrew willow he has spread the old army blanket that we have used at the beach for years. He has picked the blossom of my biggest pink geranium, put it in a mason jar and placed it in the center of the blanket. In a small soup can is the stub of a red candle.

"It's a fruit picnic," he says. "That's your place."

I get settled on the grass beside the blanket. Our plates are plastic Crisco lids. I have two strawberries, he has four.

"I have more strawberries because they're my most favorite, but I gave you the biggest apple."

"That's okay, I like apples."

We each have half a banana cut in two raggedly with a dull knife, also a few grapes and several raisins.

"We can't light the candles," he said. "We have to pretend."

I have a blue mug from the kitchen. His is brown. "That's lemonade, I squoze the lemons myself."

I take a sip and he puts his hand over his mouth and giggles. "It's just water, you know."

We could hear the soft lapping of the waves and hear the wild call of gulls. Everything shimmered in the sunlight.

"Isn't this a wonderful picnic, in the forest beside the lake?"

I look at his beautiful little face and his clear blue eyes. I am aware that things only happen once.

"Yes, Jacob Andrew, it's a wonderful picnic!"

We sit quietly for a bit, then, he jumps up. "You can put everything away," he says. "I'm going to play now."

Family Vacation

As soon as we go out the driveway our vacation begins. We're headed for Myrtle Beach, about 800 miles. It's 7:30 in the morning, my daughter Eileen is driving. She's also my best friend. I'm remembering other departures when my husband Bill, who is no longer able to go along, did all the driving. He never got lost, always knew directions. I attribute that to the fact that he used to fly those Piper Cubs all over the country. But we're OK. We're loaded with maps and all sorts of advice and we're on our way. This is a family thing. Granddaughter Andrea, her husband Mark and their three children are driving down in their van. Mark's parents, Marilyn and Ralph and brother Joe are meeting us there. We are all in the same ocean front hotel, The South Seas, but in different apartments.

We stop for the night in Charlotte. The next day we drive on secondary roads in South Carolina and I am continually amazed at the many small houses. A whole house is no bigger than my family room. Usually there is a small plot of tobacco on one side and bright flowers around a porch where occasionally someone sits in a rocking chair watching as children play in the yard or swing on an old tire. They seem proud of their houses; there's a dignity about them an unpretentiousness. I keep wondering if they are content and happy or if they long for bigger things and other places.

We arrive the second day about 2:00. I rush to the balcony. There it is! Magnificent, unending! In my mind I'm saying –

I must go down to the seas again, for the call of the running tide
Is a wild call and a clear call that may not be denied;
And all I ask is a windy day with the white clouds flying,

fragments

And the flung spray and the blown spume, and the sea-gulls crying.
John Maesfield

In the evening we walk on the beach gleaning for shark's teeth. Jacob, age five, soon becomes the shark's teeth king because he finds more than anyone. Most people haven't found any and they stop to admire his collection.

One day Mark and the kids fashion a remarkable alligator out of sand. It is six feet long with a tail twice that long (the kids get carried away, especially two-year-old Zack). They work for hours, always with an audience. Then the on-coming tide slowly takes the alligator back to the sea.

For four wonderful days my son Michael joins us. We don't see him often, and I am fearful that he will have changed. His lifestyle is more sophisticated than ours, or at least more structured. But he is just the same. His hair, which started to turn gray very early, is now silver. His complexion is just like it was at twenty. He is very knowledgeable about the Carolinas, charming and very funny. The kids love Uncle Mike.

Ralph invites us to breakfast and we all pile into his van. The kids know they are to sit on laps. They are quite unconcerned about which lap they sit on. Small lovely children, wherever they sit they are loved and welcomed.

Coming out of the Gay Dolphin one day (five floors of things you can do without) four-year-old Hannah steps on a shell which she picks up to find that it's alive. It is a hermit crab and she has already bought one that she keeps in a little box to take home. She must save this one's life! She carries it carefully in small brown hands, all the way to the hotel and places it with the other one.

Then Jacob finds a live sea urchin on the sidewalk, which he wants to take home. After his dad explains that it would surely die, they decide to put it back in the ocean. They stand at the very edge of the surf; Jacob stands on his father's shoulders and throws it as far as he can back into the sea.

We stay on the beach each night for fireworks. The exploding bright colors are no more spectacular than the people screaming, laughing and yelling from the balconies all up and down the beach.

Michael takes Eileen and me to Brookgreen Gardens, which is south of Myrtle Beach and part of the Grand Strand. It is one of the most beautiful gardens in the South, created by Archer M. Huntington in 1930 for his wife, Anna Hyatt, who was a sculptor. It is on the site of an old rice and indigo plantation, which dates from the 1700's. There are more than 500 statues, including those of his wife, by 19th and 20th century American artists.

We decided against a tour, preferring to wander around by ourselves. The statues are all life size. Many are of small endearing children. One small boy is standing on a turtle; a little girl is atop a sunflower. An old man sits on a bench reading the paper. He's very real, but he never turns a page! Many statues are of young exquisitely beautiful men and women all artfully surrounded by flowers. There is appropriate poetry engraved in marble beside some of them. The ancient live oaks with their gnarled branches laden with Spanish moss, the twisting paths, the exotic plants, small pools and fountains are mysterious and romantic. As I walk around the quiet beauty I think I must tell my poet friend about Brookgreen. It's his kind of place.

One afternoon Mike and I go to Broadway at the Beach. It is about a mile from the ocean, with more sophisticated shops, an aquarium and unusual landscaping. We do some of the shops and then go and sit on the boardwalk at a little round table and drink chocolate cokes. From across the water we hear the music of Aaron Copland's *Fanfare for the Common Man* and watch the fountain dance 50 feet in the air keeping time to the music.

fragments

Finally it's departure day. We wave good-bye to everyone, the last to leave. We decide to stop in West Virginia at Tamarack; we have the new route marked on the map which we put in the glove compartment.

After hours of driving we stop at a rest stop to check the map. Eileen points a finger; "Here's where we are. Here's where we should be. We're thirty miles off our route!"

My five foot one inch, red headed daughter stands beside the car and for three solid minutes she swears like a trooper. I take a walk.

When I come back she is crying. "It's times like this that I need Father."

I remember something I read once, and I quote, "When I fall behind she waits for me." We're silent. We sit in the car; we can't speak or risk looking at each other. Sometimes--- sometimes life is so sad.

"Enough of this," she says. She gets two cans of Pepsi out of the cooler; I break open a bag of pretzels and put Vivaldi's *Four Seasons* on the tape deck and we're off down the road.

Finally we arrive at Tamarack. It's a huge round building with pointed dormers around the roof. It looks like a humongous sunflower surrounded by trees, flowers and fountains. They call it the "art and soul of West Virginia."

We start by looking at wooden utensils, bowls and furniture. On to jewelry, clothes, toys, carpets, glass and pottery in vibrant colors. We aren't aware that we're going around in a circle until we come again to the wooden bowls. Everything is made in West Virginia.

In the center is a court where we eat luscious chicken pot pie and blackberry cobbler. We've been at Tamarack three hours and we could have stayed a day. But it is 7:00 PM

"Do you want to stop for the night? How tired are you?"

"I'm not tired, but you're doing the driving."

"Let's go for it," she says. "If we keep going we'll be home by midnight."

fragments

We stop once at a little country store where an old woman pumps gas and sells us chocolates and tells us more about her life than we really want to hear. We get home about 1:00 AM. Eileen drops me off. I go from room to room turning on lights, opening windows. It seems as if I've been gone more than two weeks. I go outside and stand beside the lake. It isn't the magnificence of the ocean, but I like the gentle lapping of the water. Since I've been away my weigela bush has burst into bloom. In the bright moonlight, under a velvet sky the white blossoms are lustrous and unreal seeming to shimmer and glow likes pearls. I breathe in the fresh scent of summer; glad to be home.

For All Eternity

A woman walks on a deserted beach. She walks aimlessly, unaware of waves splashing over her worn shoes. She is wearing blue slacks—too big—and a gray sweater hiked up in the back emphasizing the bulky figure. She wanders on down the shore and sees a building in the distance. She recognizes it as an old abandoned dance hall. She walks steadily on as if to explore. She pushes open the door, brushes away cobwebs. She stares at overturned chairs and tables thick with fallen plaster and showing signs of animals. She stands in the center of the once beautiful dance floor; a look of bewilderment comes over her tired face.

Suddenly she turns her head and listens attentively. Far off, she hears the faint strains of music. The sound comes closer. *Jeanine, I Dream of Lilac Time.* She laughs and lifts her arms above her head. *Your eyes, they beam in lilac time.* She hums the song under her breath and smoothes her lilac dress down over slim hips. The whirling lights above turn her hair to burnished gold. She turns swaying and laughing; keeping time to the music.

"I told you I'd wait."

"James! It's you!"

He takes her in his arms. They dance around and around on the polished floor. Her head on his shoulder, they glide and whirl under iridescent lights.

"Remember the bracelet you gave me? I still have it." He took it off then handed it to her.

"I remember!" She turned it over and read the inscription on the back, *for all eternity.*

"I told you I'd wait. I love you."

On the same deserted beach a young boy and girl walk quickly along, looking this way and that, searching, searching.

"She can't be very far," the boy says. "We'll find her."

"But she's so old and sometimes she gets confused."

"Do you suppose she went into that abandoned dance hall?"

"I don't think she'd go in there. It's so filthy and really dangerous with broken glass."

"We've looked every place else. Let's go in and see."

As they near the building, the girl says, "It's Jeannie! She's fallen down on the steps."

The boy kneels beside the fragile form.

"Help her up! Oh! Jeannie, what have you done to yourself?"

The boy is silent. He says gently, "It's too late, she's gone."

The girl kneels beside her, pushes the thin white hair away from the still face.

"What's in her hand?" The boy picks it up. "It looks like a bracelet. Look, it has an inscription inside. *J. through eternity.*

"I wonder where she picked that up?"

A flutter of wings rises outside the building.

Book III

Time Passes, Memories Linger

fragments

Getting Polished

I knew something was up when I came to the dinner table. Mother had all my favorite things, macaroni and cheese, dill pickles, and chocolate cake. My two older sisters were smirking at me behind Mother's back. It had to be bad news, but I thought I might as well eat my favorite meal because it could be my last. My little brother Jimmy was digging in. Nothing fazes him when there's food in front of him. I was all prepared for some scheme my parents had cooked up.

Mother said, "The way you have been running with your brothers, playing ball, dressing like the boys, well, it's actually uncouth. Your father and I have decided that beginning next Saturday morning you are going to be taking piano lessons."

"Piano lessons! Please Mom! I'll quit playing ball; I'll try to be just like my sisters."

This couldn't be happening to me! And on Saturdays, my only day to play.

"Now, don't start complaining. It's all settled. Mrs. F.W. Forney agreed to take you. The price is one dollar. Your father and I expect you to practice and make something of yourself. Money doesn't grow on trees, you know."

Jimmy kept right on shoveling mac and cheese into his mouth. Never looked up.

Mother said, "And Mrs. F.W. Forney offered to take two of you for a dollar and a half. This way you can go together and use the same music. Jimmy, you need a little polish, too. It never hurts to start young."

Jimmy looked up from his food as if he had suddenly been struck by lightning. He started to howl.

So there it was, we'd been set up. Our lives weren't our own.

Mother wakened me early on Saturday morning. She sounded cheerful.

"Time to wake up and get yourself ready for your lesson. Wear your blue gingham dress; it will look nice."

"I don't feel good, Mom." I held my hand over my stomach and pinched my arm trying to bring tears to my eyes. "You'd better call Mrs. F.W. Forney and tell her I can't start music lessons."

"That's funny," Mother said. "Jimmy seems to have a stomach problem, too." She didn't sound so cheerful now.

I knew by the sound of her voice, she meant business. We were doomed. No use to complain. All our Saturdays would be a disaster. We started off on the half mile walk to Mrs. F.W. Forney's.

"Mom said we were uncouth. What's uncouth?" Jimmy asked.

"It means we don't have any polish."

"Then after we have piano lessons, will we have couth and be polished?"

"We'll never be polished and I don't care!"

"I don't, either. Let's stay unpolished forever and ever!"

When we arrived at Mrs. F.W. Forney's, we were met by another sad kid, who took us into a small room at the back of the house right off the kitchen. There were about twelve kids shoehorned into that room. Some of the kids sat on straight chairs; others sprawled on the floor in a mess of funny papers. Everyone looked hot and unhappy.

After sitting there for about twenty minutes, Mrs. F.W. Forney came out and introduced herself. She said she hoped we'd all learn to enjoy music as much as she did. I don't know how much that was because she looked mean and unhappy. It may have been on account of the blouse she was wearing. It had a high neck with little stays on each side to hold it up. She looked like a pigeon with little legs like sticks and a big front. She wore a gold watch on a chain which she looked at quite often. I think she wanted to make sure she didn't give anyone a minute more time than they paid for. I don't believe she liked kids at all. One by one she took us into the music room where there was a piano, a long bench, and a funny black kind of box that she said was a metronome.

I could tell that everyone wanted to be some place else except one girl. She looked to be about nine, same as me. Her name was Marjorie. She was wearing a bright pink dress with a wide sash tied in the back in a big bow. The ribbons in her yellow curls matched her dress. Her knee socks had lace around the top. Yuck!

Jimmy and I shared one of the straight chairs as we waited our turn. He held tight to my hand. Sometimes we waited a half hour or more for our turn. Saturday after Saturday, we dragged ourselves to Mrs. F.W. Forney's. The same funny papers were there week after week. Some were so torn you couldn't read them. Once in a while, one would be replaced by a new one. Then it was a fight to see who could get there first.

Sitting there I thought about all the things I could be doing. I could be riding my bike, swimming in the creek, or just sitting there thinking about stuff. I could hear lucky kids outside playing jump rope.

Mother, Mother, I am sick,
Send for the doctor, quick, quick, quick.
Doctor, Doctor, will I die?
Yes, my darling,
By and by.
How many coaches will I have?
Enough for you and

Your family, too.
1-2-3-4-

Heck, I could go to 100! Oh, it was sickening. Here we are trying to get polished.

We soon learned about the metronome. I hated that metronome! It just kept right on going 1-2, 1-2, 1-2 . It didn't care if you missed a note or played the wrong one or stopped and started over.

After a couple of weeks Mrs. F.W. Forney came out with her arms around Marjorie. "You all started at the same time. Now I want you to hear Marjorie play *The Happy Farmer.*"

Marjorie smiled in a stuck-up kind of way. I really can't stand her. Jimmy and I are still struggling with *Every Good Boy Does Fine* and she is already playing *The Happy Farmer.*

"Is she polished now?" Jimmy asked.

"I don't know. Who cares anyway?"

Mrs. F.W. Forney never allowed anyone to go to the bathroom. She said we should go before we come because there are too many of use to go traipsing through her house, and besides her husband can't be annoyed.

One Saturday we were sitting in the funny paper room, I on one side and Jimmy on the other, right across from me. It was hot and sticky. Everyone was grumpy (except Marjorie, of course).

Jimmy was wiggling and he looked like he'd fall asleep any minute. I remember once Jimmy was chosen to sing a solo at church. For a little kid, he was a really good singer. As he stood up there on that stage, he kept wiggling and didn't start to sing, although the woman playing the piano started a couple of times. Mother knew exactly what was wrong. She walked right up to that stage, picked Jimmy up and said, "We'll be back in a minute." She took him to the bathroom, brought him back, and stood him on the stage. He sang his song right through, and the crowd clapped more for Jimmy than for anyone else. My mother is smart in lots of ways.

Jimmy was nodding. That metronome is enough to hypnotize you. 1-2, 1-2, 1-2. Suddenly, Jimmy falls head first right into the funny papers. And then to make it even worse, he wets his pants. I was so mad! I glared at everyone in the room. They didn't dare laugh.

I said, "I'm outta here!" I picked Jimmy up and carried him out of there. My little brother! Nobody is gonna make fun of him. I didn't tell Mother he wet his pants. I think she could tell anyway.

"Now I'll never have any couth," Jimmy said between sobs.

"You don't need to have any couth, you're just right the way you are."

That was the end of our musical careers. I never even learned to play *The Happy Farmer.* I tried not to look too happy when Mother said we could quit.

But Mother was undaunted. The thought of giving up never even entered her head. She did let Jimmy off the hook. She'd work on him later. But for me, she had another surprise. I didn't think anything could be worse than those piano lessons. But I was wrong.

Mother and her friend, Mrs. Cletis Handshoe, were in the living room with the door closed. That was a bad sign right there. I hoped it wasn't about me. Maybe she had waited too long to get me polished.

Then she opened the door and called me in. I knew Mrs. Cletis Handshoe. She lived in our neighborhood. She is old; I think she was born old. She is a big lady, way bigger than my mother, who is little and pretty, most of the time.

Mother was smiling. "Mrs. Cletis Handshoe has decided to give elocution lessons and she'd like you to be her first pupil." Mother said it like it was a great honor.

"What's elocution?" I asked. I hoped maybe it was swimming or some sort of exercising since Mrs. Cletis Handshoe coulda used some of that herself. At this point I wasn't too upset.

"It's learning to speak properly," Mother said.

"Is this some more of that couth business?" I asked bitterly.

"I'm sure you'll like it better than the music lessons. Besides, Mrs. Cletis Handshoe will come here on Saturday mornings. She'll find a poem for you and bring it over tomorrow. Then you'll have time to learn at least part of it by next week."

Maybe it won't be too bad, I thought. I know lots of poetry already like *How do you like to go up in a swing* or *I have a little shadow that goes in and out with me*, or *the fog comes on little cat feet*. I can do this. It will be easy.

Then Mrs. Cletis Handshoe brought my poem. *The Spell of the Yukon* by Robert W. Service. Where did she dig this up? What's the Yukon anyway? I read it over.

I wanted the gold, and I sought it:
I scrabbled and mucked like a slave.
Was it famine or scurvy, I fought it;
I hurled my youth into a grave.
I wanted the gold and got it-
Came out with a fortune last fall,
Yet somehow life's not what I thought it,
And somehow the gold isn't all.

I didn't know what it was all about, but I memorized the first verse. Now I could say that in a couple of minutes and be out of there.

On Saturday I didn't get dressed up. After all Mrs. Cletis Handshoe was coming to my house, and I'd be out of there in a few minutes. I'd have the whole day to play outside.

As soon as I said hello to Mrs. Cletis Handshoe, I started right in on my poem. "I wanted the gold and I sought it."

"Wait, wait just a minute. There's more to elocution than that! Now stand, don't slouch. Hands down at your sides. Now say, 'My poem is *The Spell of the Yukon* by Robert W. Service.' Let your audience think about that for a second or two. Now, start your poem."

My audience was huddled by the door, my two sisters, two brothers, and my mother.

"I wanted the gold and I sought it."

"With gestures," said Mrs. Cletis Handshoe.

I waved both hands in the air.

"I scrabbled and mucked like a slave."

"Gestures, gestures!" Mrs. Cletis Handshoe shouted. "Now, repeat that last line."

How do you scrabble and muck?

"I scrabbled and mucked like a slave," I repeated.

"Gestures, gestures!"

I used both fists and fought scurvy.

"I hurled my youth into a grave."

I hurled myself onto the floor and tried to look dead.

Well, this was too much from my mother. She started to laugh, and when my mother laughs, everyone laughs. She giggles and once she starts, she can't stop. Mrs. Cletis Handshoe looked really mad. Then my audience started to laugh. Jimmy and I forgot all about getting polished and laughed, too. Then Mrs. Cletis Handshoe laughed the hardest of all.

Mother made tea and brought out some fat ginger cookies and we had a kind of party that Saturday morning. And laughter, like light, filled the old kitchen.

I guess Jimmy and I never did get polished.

The Operation

"Uncle Doc says they gotta come out, and he's gonna do us all at once and get it over with," Lu says. She is eleven, and when you are eleven, going on twelve, you know lots of things. "And," she continues, "he's going to do it in the kitchen."

"Why's he doing it in the kitchen?" Milt asks.

"Cause Uncle Doc does us for nothing, that's why."

So here we are all huddled at the top of the steps, the girls in long white nightgowns and the boys in blue-striped pajamas.

Sophie is sitting in her big old rocking chair in the hall at the top of the steps. She is watching us. She knows exactly what is going on, but she doesn't say much. Her face shines softly in the light. She has been with us forever, we love Sophie.

The back steps go down into a big kitchen. Dad painted the walls on each side of the stairs a dark green. This is our chalkboard. It is covered with lop-sided purple houses, strange looking green animals with too many legs and big staring eyes. There is a list of spelling words in a neat column, and some crooked numbers left there by Milt. Our colored chalk and erasers are on a shelf below the railing. The steps are oak, worn pale and dull from frequent washings. It is a place where we can draw, eat cookies, spill juice, and make a mess. Our own place.

The big square oak table in the kitchen has been covered with white sheets, and Uncle Doc's instruments are on the counter beside the sink.

Lu will go down first, then Marty, age ten. I'm next: I'm six. Then Milt, age five and Jimmy, only three.

"Why do we have to have our adenoids out anyway?" Milt asks.

"Dad says we can't breathe right with adenoids and our mouths will hang open and people will think we can't even tie our own shoes," I answer.

"I know people with their mouths open. I saw them in church and their eyes were shut," Marty says.

"That's different," Lu says. "They were asleep."

"Nobody's getting mine out," Marty says. "I'm not going down. They can't make me."

"Uncle Doc says they gotta come out."

"I don't know care what Uncle Doc says. Nobody's getting mine."

"Dad says we'd look like we had only one oar in the water."

"We don't even have a boat so it won't matter."

"Can they tie their own shoes?" Jimmy asks.

"Who?"

"The people in church."

"I don't know. Ask Uncle Doc."

"What are adenoids anyway?"

"They're big old things that grow in your throat."

"How big are they?"

"I think they're as big as a marble."

"I think they're as big as your eye."

"What are they good for?"

"They aren't good for nothin'," Milt says.

"Then why do we have them if they aren't any good?"

"Somebody goofed, that's what I think."

"They aren't getting mine," Marty says.

"Uncle Doc says they gotta come out."

"Quit telling me about Uncle Doc. *HE'*s not getting mine!"

"You won't get any ice cream."

"Can I tie my own shoes after he gets mine?" Jimmy asks.

"Maybe not right away. I'll help you, I can tie my shoes," says Milt.

"Are you scared, Milt?" I ask.

"No, I'm not scared. Nothin' scares me. I'll go right down and jump up on the table by myself."

"Then why did you wet your pants if you aren't scared?"

"Didn't wet my pants."

"Yes you did."

"Did not."

"Liar!"

"Is it gonna hurt?"

"It won't hurt a bit; we'll be asleep."

"We just got up; we're not tired."

"Uncle Doc will make you go to sleep. He has this thing that smells bad and he puts it over your face and in a minute you're asleep."

"When you wake up, your adenoids are gone."

"And then you get ice cream. Mama said we'd get ice cream. I'm gonna get strawberry. What are you going to get, Marty?"

"Uncle Doc's not getting mine. I'm not going down."

"Then you won't get ice cream."

"I don't care; he's not getting mine."

"What does he do with them?"

"Do with what?"

"All those adenoids?"

"He throws them in the garbage."

"Maybe he keeps them in a bottle."

"He'd have too many; he does lots of people."

"So they can all tie their own shoes?"

Sophie, who has been quietly listening to this discussion about adenoids, stands up, puts her hand on Lu's shoulder and says, "It's time for you to go down, Honey. Doctor is ready for you. Be a good girl now, hold on to the railing so you don't fall."

fragments

Lu is brave, she's old already. She holds on tight to the railing. I see her legs shaking but she doesn't cry, just walks right down, and Dad opens the door at the bottom of the steps.

We can hear Uncle Doc. "Right up on the table. That's fine. It isn't going to hurt. You won't even feel it."

The door closes. We smell something terrible. We can't hear anything at all.

"I'm not going down; they can't make me." Marty is crying because she knows she is next.

"Uncle Doc says they gotta come out!"

"I hate Uncle Doc!"

"You won't get any ice cream."

"I don't care if I never get any ice cream."

"It isn't gonna hurt. Mama said it wouldn't hurt."

Sophie takes Marty's hand. "It's your turn. Go down just like your sister did."

Marty screams and holds on to the railing. Her long curly hair is in a tangle. Between sobs and hiccups she screams, "No, no, no. You're not getting mine."

"Doc is ready for you, Marty," Dad says, "no use crying and carrying on. It'll be over before you know it."

He comes up the steps, takes her hands off the railing and carries her down, kicking and screaming.

Then Sophie says, "you're next, Wilma."

I can't move. I hang on to the railing with both hands. I think I may die. My heart will pound right out of me. I can't scream or cry or even whimper. My legs feel like wet cornflakes. I don't know my own name. The steps in front of me are so long, so steep. The walls are going to fold in on me. Then I hear Dad's voice. It seems to come from far away. "Come on, Uncle Doc is waiting." I can tie my own shoes, not so good, but pretty good. Then I slowly, carefully put one foot in front of the other and Dad lifts me up and puts me on the table.

fragments

The next thing I know I'm in bed with Milt and Jimmie. Mother is standing beside us, smiling. "Now that wasn't so bad, was it?"

"They said it wouldn't hurt!" Milt says.

"You gonna have ice cream?" I whisper.

"Let's wait till tomorrow."

Fragments

I knew a woman, Mrs. French who did housework for half the people in our town. She was little and wiry with thin white hair. She was about five feet tall, talked all the time, and jumped around like a squirrel. But she was a good worker so most people put up with her chatter.

It was a very hot summer and Mrs. French remarked to someone that she never suffered from the heat because she just stripped naked and slept out on her porch. That summer, all the boys made frequent trips up and down in front of Mrs. French's house. No one actually ever saw Mrs. French stark naked on her porch but we knew it was true. Hadn't she said so herself?

Old Josie sits on the stoop in front of her house all scrunched up like a little old gnome and contemplates the world through bleary eyes. She lives on the wrong side of town in a little unpainted house. It is fronted on the sidewalk without a porch so that she sits on the stoop with her feet on the sidewalk. She wears men's shoes which are much too large for her and heavy black socks. She never wears a coat, just layers and layers of clothes, all dark and ragged. Her hair is white and quite short.

When I was about eight years old, two other little girls and I went to visit Old Josie. The first time we went on a dare. Then later we were interested in the way she lived. Her house was small, and as she sat on the stoop in front of the open door, we could see the dark, sparsely furnished

125

room with the bed in the corner, the rocking chair, the rag rug, the stove, and a round table with one chair.

We went to see her several times a week that year. She told us she came from the "Old Country." She was always alone. We couldn't understand much of what she said but she was pleased to see us. Once there was a woman in the house who seemed to be cleaning, sweeping, shaking the rug and cooking something on the small stove.

"Is Josie your mother?" I asked.

"No, no relation."

"Does she have any children?"

"No children, no one."

"Doesn't she have friends?"

"No friends, none at all.'"

"Now she does," I said. "She has us!"

"Well, yes, I guess she does."

Sometimes we shared a piece of candy with Josie or a cookie left over from our lunch. She'd laugh and clap her hands. One day she wasn't sitting in her usual place. I knocked on the door. The same woman was there. She said, "Josie is sick."

"Can we see her?"

"No, she's too sick. Run along!"

The next day we were back. The woman came to the door again.

"Is she better?" we asked.

"No, she's dying."

"Could we see her? Please, could we see her? We're her friends.'"

"Well," the woman hesitated, "Yes, I guess it will be alright. But just for a minute now, hear?"

We went in, the three of us, and stood beside the bed. We were frightened. She looked so small in the big bed. She wore a white night gown with a high neck and long sleeves. She appeared to be asleep.

fragments

"Your little friends are here," the woman said.

Josie opened her eyes and looked at each one of us. Then she reached out her hand. I had never even touched her. Now I took her hand in my small one. It felt cool, like a bird about to flutter away. She nodded her head and closed her eyes. In that instant there was an awareness in our eight-year-old minds that people get old and die, an awareness of our own mortality. We went home without speaking.

The next day when we came back there was a wreath on the closed door.

In my town, there's an old red brick house, high on a hill. It is surrounded by a brick wall. In the center are narrow, almost-concealed steps leading up to the house.

On a summer night, a woman is usually sitting on the steps. She wears a flowing white nightgown and is in her bare feet. Her pale hair frames a beautiful face. When anyone comes along, friend or stranger, she gets up and walks beside them.

When she suddenly appeared beside me, apparently out of nowhere, it was heart-stopping! With her hair shimmering like a halo around her face, she was ethereal and unreal. She said her name was Moonbeam.

My first encounter with Moonbeam was frightening and I avoided that side of the street for a long time. Later, I told a friend about my experience. She laughed and said, "Oh you needn't be afraid of her. She has lived there for years. Her name is Theodosia De Armett. She comes out at night, never goes far from home."

I walked with her many times after that and actually looked forward to it.

fragments

No one comes from Social Services. No one recommends a psychiatrist. No one threatens to have her removed to a safer place. If she wants to walk around at night in her nightgown and call herself Moonbeam, it is her business. In our town, we accept her the way she is.

fragments

The Rowlands

Dad announces that we are going to the Rowlands. Just that word *Rowlands* and we are wild with excitement. There are six Hartley kids and six Rowland cousins. My cousin Pinkie is my age—seven, going on eight. We're soul mates.

It takes a whole day to get there where Uncle Doc has just started to be a doctor in a new town, and so far I don't think he's doing very well. I guess he's busy with lots of sick people. But they pay him in stuff, like bushels of potatoes, which are okay, and turnips and parsnips that you have to get used to. Sometimes, he gets apples. Apples are always good; no matter what kind, you can't beat an apple. But a little money is what he really needs.

We load the Studebaker, three girls in the back. I always have to sit in the middle because I'm the youngest girl. My brothers Milt and Jimmy sit on the little seats that fold up from the floor. Charlie sits on Mother's knee in the front seat with Dad.

The Rowlands have a big old house right in the center of town. Of course it had to be big with all those kids. There's only one thing I don't like about the Rowlands. All of the kids, except Pinkie, are bed wetters. Well, I don't really care, but because there are so many of us, we have to sleep three in a bed. If I'm lucky, I get to sleep on the edge with Pinkie in the middle. But if Mary gets in the middle, too bad!

In the morning Aunt Beth gathers up all the bedding, and the next night everything is fresh and clean. Now that's one thing I don't understand. Uncle Doc should be able to do something. My father owns a hardware store, and none of the Hartleys are bed wetters. So, what's wrong with the Rowlands? It's Uncle Doc's fault if you ask me.

You have to see the rooms in the house to believe it. They're huge! And it's a good thing, too, because they have a rolly coaster right in their house. A man brought his three kids into Uncle Doc's office and wanted their tonsils taken out all on the same day. "Get it over with," he said. Then, instead of money, he gave Uncle Doc the rolly coaster. He brought it home and set it up in the house because they don't have a yard. The *three tonsil rolly coaster* starts in the kitchen. You go up a ladder about as tall as my dad, get on a little car and start down. You go all the way through the kitchen, gathering speed into the dining room, just missing the long oak table and zoom into the living room past the bookcase, past the table with the antique lamp, and finally zip into a rolled up rug. It's wild!

My mother and Aunt Beth don't seem to mind at all. They just go on baking pies and cakes, fixing vegetables, and laughing. Mother and Aunt Beth love being together. They're sisters, you know. They're old, I spose they're forty. But, the *three tonsil rolly coaster* doesn't bother them at all.

On a warm, sunlit day Pinkie and I decide to go across the street to the high school building where there's a sprinkler watering the lawn. We can run through the sprinkler and lie on the cool grass.

I ran through first. I love Pinkie, but she's a little wimpy sometimes. I'm not sure she'll run through the sprinkler.

"I made a rainbow!" I shout.

"You couldn't make a rainbow. God made the rainbow!"

"Not this one. I made it myself. I'll go through again just to be sure." I ran through. "There it is. All those lovely colors! You go through, you'll see."

Pinkie gets up her courage and runs through. "I saw it. I saw it!"

"I told you."

"I thought God made the rainbow and promised there'd never be another flood." Pinkie is almost crying.

"Well, there's been another flood! It was in our basement. I should know because it ruined Charlie's biggest Teddy Bear and my father's leather boots and Marty's winter jacket."

"Maybe God didn't know about your basement. Maybe he wasn't there," Pinkie said.

"I thought He was everywhere. That's what Mrs. Chamberlin said in Sunday School."

"Maybe He was too busy that day. You know, the whole big world..."

"Probly."

"Maybe He made half a promise."

"No, I think He made a promise, but maybe He didn't know about sprinklers."

"Are we gonna tell anybody about our rainbow?"

"Let's keep it a secret."

"Are we going to make a promise on our rainbow?" Pinkie asks. "I think we should."

"What are you going to promise?"

I have to think about it. "I know! I'm never, ever, going to get algebra."

"What's algebra?"

"I don't know what it is, but my friend in high school says it stinks and if anyone ever mentions algebra, just run the other way and don't look back!"

"Can I have part of your promise? I never want algebra, either."

"Sure you can. We made our rainbow together."

"Maybe the rainbow story is like the stork story."

"Yeah!" Pinkie says, "I know that isn't true. My dad delivers babies all the time and I watch him getting ready to go. I've never, ever, not even once, seen a stork in the car with him."

"Maybe the stork goes on ahead."

"Then, why would my dad have to go if the baby is already delivered?"

"I think it's a story someone made up to fool little kids. That's what I think."

"Probly."

"Your father looks like a stork!" I say. We both giggle. Uncle Doc has a long nose, and when he wears his big black coat and walks funny, to make us laugh, he looks like a stork.

Dinnertime at the Rowlands is just about the best thing that ever happens. There's a table big enough for all the kids and our mothers and fathers. I told you the rooms were big! Of course, Mother and Aunt Beth jump up and down a lot, taking care of everyone. There's a white tablecloth on the table, and we each have our own napkin. When we are through eating, we fold our napkin beside our place ready for the next meal.

And oh, the food! Great mounds of mashed potatoes, heaping dishes of yellow rutabagas, corn, green beans, carrots, tomatoes, and smaller dishes of cottage cheese, homemade pickles, applesauce, strawberry jam, and warm, crusty bread. Always there's fried chicken, ham, and roast beef. And desserts! It's like you've gone to heaven!

Sometimes, somebody makes a mess. Charlie spilled his milk all over the white tablecloth. Aunt Beth quickly mopped it up, told Charlie it was okay, and brought a clean towel to put under his plate. Charlie's big blue eyes were brimming with tears. He's my beautiful little brother. I couldn't bear to see him cry.

"Oh, Mother," I say, "I just got strawberry jam on the tablecloth."

"I'm so stupid," Danny says, "I spilled the gravy."

Charlie starts to smile. He isn't the only one! Then everyone laughs.

The men never help with the meal, just sit and enjoy themselves. But after dinner my dad and Uncle Doc and the oldest boy cousins do all the dishes. They wear big blue aprons and shoo everyone else out of the kitchen. That's pretty nice if you ask me.

Suddenly in the middle of the meal, just for a minute, I'm sad. I don't understand it. It is a sort of emptiness. Something I can't name. I look at the faces of all my brothers and sisters, and I look at all my cousins. I want this day to never end. But even if I'm only seven, going on eight, I know it won't last. I wonder what it will be like when we're all big. Will we still love to be together?

Then, just as suddenly, I'm happy again, and laughing with Pinkie.

fragments

William

Third grade was the year we were into jumping rope. If anyone asked us to play ball or run races, we'd say we're not into that this year. You had to be into *something*. This year it was jumping rope. So at recess (the only really important thing) Mil, Rita, Naomi, Julia, and I get out the jump rope. It is a piece of clothes line, all frayed at the ends. It is our favorite rope. It makes you jump higher and longer than any other rope. I take one end and Rita, the other. Naomi won't take her turn. She is afraid she'll do it wrong. She is afraid of almost everything. As we turn the rope, it sends up little puffs of dust and makes a soft plopping sound. Mil is very good. She can jump up to thirty every time.

"Here comes William. Let's give him the next turn," I say.

William is Julia's little brother. He is in second grade. Their father died before Julia can remember. There is a younger brother Robert at home. Julia's mother teaches first grade.

The rope goes faster and faster and William jumps in. We all chant, "One potato, two potato, three potato, four, five potato, six potato, seven potato, more, 1, 2, 3, 4 ..."

"Oh William, you are the best rope jumper in the whole second grade."

William, hair the color of wild honey, sparkling blue eyes, is all smiles. He is so proud of himself; his heart sings. And in that moment I decide I am going to marry William. He is a year younger than me, but that won't make any difference once we are big.

After school we walk home together, Mil, Rita, Naomi, Julia, and I. We walk down the old railroad tracks. We wait

fragments

for William. Today is Friday, the day we each have a nickel to go to Cidermans and buy candy. The best thing about Cidermans is standing at the long glass case and looking at the chocolate bars, the Necco Sweets, the jaw breakers, the all-day suckers, the licorice sticks. It is so hard to make the right decision!

"Come on, William, hurry up; we're going to Cidermans."

William hangs back. He's kicking the gravel between the rails. He looks like he is about to cry.

"What's wrong with you, William? Don't you feel good?" Julia asks.

"I can't go; go on without me."

"Don't you want to go with us?"

"I lost my nickel," he says.

I think about that for a minute. Then I say, "I'm for getting a Clark bar. I've already decided. I'll give you a piece of mine."

"Me, too, I'm getting a Clark bar," Rita says.

"Me, too," from Mil.

"Me, too," Naomi says.

And Julia agrees.

"You'll have the biggest Clark bar of all!" I say.

"Can you really do that?" he asks.

"Course we can!"

William is all smiles now. He scampers ahead, balancing easily on the rails, filled with the kind of joy that happens when you are seven or eight and on your way to Cidermans.

Naomi doesn't want to walk on the rails; she is afraid she'll fall off. But we say we'll help her. Mil goes ahead, and I follow.

"You're doing great, Naomi. You only fell off once."

fragments

On Monday William isn't with Julia. "William didn't feel good so he stayed home. Uncle Doc is going to look in on him later today," Julia informs us. Dr. Hartford is Julia's uncle. He lives a few blocks from Julia.

Tuesday, Julia isn't at school. Julia's mother isn't at school, either.

On Wednesday Julia is back. "William has Scarlet Fever," she says. "Robert and I had to move to Uncle Doc and Aunt Jane's house. William is quarantined."

"What's quarantined?"

"I'll show you after school."

Mil, Rita, Naomi, and I go home with Julia. We don't know what to expect. There on the front of Julia's house, right beside the front door is a huge red sign, *Quarantined.*

"Nobody can go in or out except Uncle Doc," Julia informs us.

"Who takes care of William?"

"Mother stays in there with him. She can't come out until he's better."

"How can she go to the store to buy food?"

"People bring lots of food. They put it on the porch, and Mother comes out and gets it," Julia says.

Julia's mother comes to the door and waves.

"Where's William?" I ask.

"He's upstairs in his bedroom. Come over to the side and we can see him."

We all troop around to the side of the house and there's William at the window. He looks small and unhappy, but he waves.

William's teacher tells the children that William has Scarlet Fever; that it may take a long time for him to get better. She writes Scarlet Fever on the blackboard. She tells the children they may write letters to William and she'll give them to Julia.

fragments

Day after day we deliver the letters. We read some of them on our way home. Here are some of William's letters:

> Get well, I have nobody to eat with,
> > your pal, Danny

> You are the best jump roper. Come back soon,
> > your friend Sam.

> Your seat is empty. It don't seem right,
> > signed Tim.

> I miss your funny face. Hurry back,
> > your friend Mary

> You can use my crayons, the good ones,
> > your friend Alice.

> Does Scarlet Fever hurt? I don't like stuff that hurts. I had a toothache once,
> > your friend Molly.

> I never liked you much but I don't want you to be sick. I'll be your friend when you come back,
> > signed Joe.

William has a small basket tied to a rope. He lowers it out the window. Julia puts the letters in the basket very carefully. She doesn't touch the rope or the basket. We wait until William pulls the basket up and into his room. He stands there a minute and waves and smiles. It is a sad little smile. Sometimes it makes us cry.

It seems to go on for weeks. The teacher explains that Scarlet Fever takes a long time to get better.

Then one day Julia isn't at school. Our teacher says she has something to tell us. Miss Baumann, who is usually smiling, looks like she has been crying. We are silent and scared. Big people aren't supposed to cry.

Then she says, "William died in the night. He was too sick and the doctor couldn't make him better."

It was a terrible day. We all cried. The teacher cried, too. Mrs. Evereet the principal came in and talked to us. I don't remember what she said. I don't remember the rest of the day. It just couldn't be true. My grandmother was almost one hundred. William was only seven! You don't die when you're seven. Do you?

Julia and Robert move back home. The Quarantine sign was taken down. The next week Julia was back in school. We all walk together down the tracks. We don't care about balancing on the rails, we don't jump rope at recess. We don't go to Cidermans on Friday.

Every day after school I go over to be with Julia.

"Why don't you go and play with some of your other little friends?" Mother says. "You've been at Julia's every day. I hate to see you so sad."

"Julia needs me," I say. I stand by the screen door, moving back and forth. I don't know what to do. The day is so beautiful; a sweet breeze blows my hair off my face. It smells like spring. Suddenly, the world is too much.

"Don't go today, dear, come and help me make cookies," Mother says.

"I have to go. Julia needs me."

"You've done all you can for Julia. You can't help her anymore."

I hesitate a moment, then I whisper, "I can help her cry."

fragments

Sunday Rides

It is Sunday afternoon; it's the day Dad always takes us for a ride.

"When are we going?" Charlie asks.

"As soon as your father gets home with the car," Mother says.

"What's wrong with the car?"

"Nothing's wrong with it. He just took it to Columbiana yesterday to get it painted. He couldn't pick it up on Saturday, you know, because he is at the store, late. So he's getting it today."

"What color will it be?" Charlie asks.

"The same color, dark green, but it will look brand new."

"Then we'll go for a ride?"

"Yes, but it will be quite a while. Why don't you go outside and play with your cars and little animals?"

My brother Charlie is three years old. He's gotta be the best looking little guy in the whole town, maybe in the whole world. When you look into his eyes, it seems like he remembers wondrous things that happened before he was born. Charlie is the reason I like to get up in the morning. And I'm not the only one. It's that way with the whole family.

The boys keep running pell-mell through the house, in and out the back door. They aren't a bit good at waiting or being quiet. I guess maybe that's because they're boys. Mother always yells, "Don't slam the door!" Then the door slams. I think she just says that whenever she sees them.

She knows it will slam. I don't think she cares. It's just what mothers do.

On Sunday afternoon, Dad always takes us someplace. We all pile into the big Studebaker and go just anywhere. Dad never tells us where we're going. Sometimes we take the red brick road that goes to Columbiana. It goes through Negley, and on to Columbiana. Dad always tells us to keep our eyes open or we'll miss Negley. It makes us feel like we are from the big city ourselves although East Palestine isn't a whole lot better, to tell the truth. We call the route the "Columbiana Bricks". It's our least favorite place to go for a ride.

Sometimes he turns the other way, and we go to Pennsylvania. Pennsylvania is real adventurous. That's because Pennsylvania drivers are dangerous, and the men are mean. The reason we know this is because Dad bumped a man's car once, and the car slid off the road. Dad got right out of the car to make sure no one was hurt. But the driver of the Pennsylvania car jumped out shaking his fist telling Dad just what he was going to do to him. And he used lots of swear words. The man's wife just sat in the car with her head down.

Dad said, "Is your wife hurt?"

"We're going to settle this first," the man yelled.

"I'll take care of your car," Dad said, "but for Heaven's sake, Man, aren't you concerned about your wife?"

You can see why we don't think very highly of Pennsylvania men.

But there are good things about Pennsylvania. We have relatives there, and they always make us welcome. They live in this big house with many porches. These four ladies are sisters. They are my mother's second cousins. Mother says their father had lots of money, and he left them enough that they never have to work. But they are always busy doing something for people who need help. What I like about them is that they are always laughing. I think maybe it's because they have all that money. They always ask us to stay for dinner. Mother says that we almost never get asked to eat because there are too many of us. I suppose she didn't think of that before she had all of us. I can see where it would be sort of inconvenient to have nine people drop in for a meal. But the cousins in Pennsylvania actually coax us to stay.

We also like to go to Waterford, Ohio. Aunt Mary Chain lives there. Her house sits on a hill. We park on the street, climb up fifteen steps, rest on a little open space, and then climb up fifteen more steps. Aunt Mary Chain's little brown house is perched on top. It has a porch that is just big enough for one chair. On nice days she sits on her porch, and she says she can see the whole world from there. Pink roses climb up both sides of it all summer, and it almost seems like a story book house. She always offers us cookies, but Dad has told us to say that we aren't hungry even though we're always ready to eat. I think she doesn't have enough money, even for herself. Sometimes I see Dad tucking something into her apron pocket. She pats Dad's hand and smiles. Aunt Mary Chain is a sweet lady. She loves my mother. My mother is named after her—they are both Marys.

With all the adventurous places to go, I hope we don't go out the "Columbiana Bricks." We just go to Columbiana, and then turn around and come back. Of course, just riding in the car is always exciting. I look at all the houses and wonder who lives there, and think about how it would be if I lived there. Would I have my own room? Would I ride the school bus? Could I have animals? I like the smells of summer—the orchards, the flowers, the animals, and the hot tar on the roads. On those rides the world seems so big and scary. I want to go every place and see everything, but I feel safe and snug in the car.

"Your father's here," Mother calls. "Get Charlie and get in the car. Hurry now, we're ready to go."

"Where's Charlie?"

"He's in the back yard playing with his toys."

I go out the back door. "It's time to go, Charlie. Come get in the car."

Charlie isn't in the back yard. He must be inside. I call him and look everywhere. Charlie loves to hide and have everyone hunting for him. Then he laughs when he is found in some very obvious place.

But I can't find him, and Dad is waiting for us.

"I can't find Charlie," I tell Mother.

Mother smiles and tells my three sisters and the boys that Charlie is hiding. We all go from room to room calling him. He'll come out now and laugh, and then we'll all get in the car.

Finally, Dad comes to see what is going on. We really can't find Charlie anywhere. Dad is alarmed now. It's the worst feeling I've ever had in my whole life. I'm scared! What would we do without Charlie? My sisters are crying; the boys are unnaturally quiet. I can't even look at Mother.

Dad calls Mr. Harvey, our friend. He is a policeman.

"We'll find him," he says. "He can't have gone very far. I'll take several men with me and we'll scour the neighborhood. Everyone knows Charlie. He'll be all right."

Then we spend the worst three hours I have ever known. I can't live without Charlie. We don't talk to each other or try to help each other. What can we do? We just sit and wait and wait and wait.

fragments

Then, when it seems we can't bear it another minute, Mr. Harvey calls.

"I've found him! He's fine!" Mr. Harvey laughs. "He was on the road to Columbiana, about a mile away. He was pulling his red wagon. He said he was taking it to get it painted."

The next day Dad took Charlie to Columbiana, and got his wagon painted.

It looks brand new!

fragments

The Bed

"Let's go down to Grandfather's and play in the barn. We can feed the pony and jump in the hay mow." I suggested.

"Okay, I guess," Mil said, "but we did that yesterday. Let's think of something different."

Mil and I had been best friends since first grade. Now that we were nine years old we knew ever so much more about everything.

Grandfather's house was only a block from my house so we started off.

We called "hello" to Aunt Mary Warner, who lived across from Grandfather's, and carefully avoided Mrs. Hoffmeister's iron fence because once she called the police when we swung on it. We didn't hurt her old fence!

Behind Grandfather's house, close beside the barn, was the shop. It was a large brown building with heavy sliding doors.

"What's in there?" Mil asked.

"Nothing now. Grandfather used it a long time ago. He buries people, you know."

"Can we go in? It isn't locked, is it?"

"I don't think so. Let's try the door."

We both pushed the door until it rumbled open. We stepped inside.

The large room was empty except for about a dozen folding chairs and a long table. It smelled of old wood and dust and, faintly, of disinfectant like it had been cleaned a long time ago and then closed up. Cobwebs hanging from the ceiling made the room feel weird and uncomfortable.

144

fragments

We stood close together just inside the door, hesitant and wide-eyed.

"Is this where your Grandfather ...?"

"Yes, but not any more. He has another place now. Mother told me that once a long time ago, when lots of people died of the flu, Grandfather had seven people in here waiting to be buried!"

"Oh, this place has gotta be haunted!" Mil said.

"Anyway, that was a long time ago. There's nothing in here now!"

"I know that. But just think, all those people long ago before we were born even! Do you believe in ghosts?"

"Not really!"

"But, don't you feel kinda funny?"

"Kinda."

"What's in that other room?" Mil asked.

"That's always locked. Nobody is ever allowed in there. But we can look in the little window at the top of the door."

We stood on tiptoe and looked into a small room. We could see shelves on one wall where there were large bottles of different sizes, some brown glass, some clear.

"What's in those bottles?" Mil asked.

"I don't know. I don't want to know, either."

"What's upstairs?" Mil asked.

"I can't remember much about being up there. Let's go up and see. Just old stuff, I think."

At the top of the stairs, another heavy door. We pushed it open and looked inside. Dust motes swam in the shafts of sunlight coming through one small window, making it seem like we were looking through frosted glass. It smelled of old wood and just faintly of flowers and perfume.

"What are those funny little boxes?" Mil asked.

We looked at brown wooden boxes, no longer than my arm, and rounded on each end. Carved on the top of each one, a small angel.

"Those are baby caskets. Grandfather will line them with pale blue or pink satin and soft pillows. He used to give me leftover scraps for my dolls."

"Oh! That's so sweet," Mil said, as she traced her finger lovingly over the angels.

"What's over there under that tarp?"

We pushed it off and uncovered what looked to be stacks of wood. But on closer inspection, it appeared to be parts of furniture. We started pulling pieces out.

"Oh look, here's part of a bed," Mil said. "It's the head of a bed, not broken or anything."

"Let's see if all the pieces are here. Maybe it's not a real bed."

We moved pieces to one side until we had uncovered the head and foot and side rails of a low bed. We rubbed off some of the black dirt and found beautiful dark wood.

"Oh look, Mil, another bed under here. A four-poster! Hurry, let's see if it's all here."

We stood the head of the four-poster up. The posts were taller than me. It looked like one big round ball after another until the top one ended in a point. It was so beautiful! I'd never seen a bed like that. I'd feel like a princess in that bed. I could ask Grandmother for one of her lovely old quilts, maybe the blue and white one. I wanted that bed more than anything.

"Where did these beds come from?" Mil asked. "Are you allowed to have them? It's so romantic finding them here in this strange place."

"I'll have to ask Grandfather."

"You go ask then. I'll stay here and find the other pieces. But don't be long. I don't want to be up here alone."

Grandfather was sitting at his desk, working on his books. But he never cared if I interrupted him.

"Mil and I were upstairs in the shop, and we found two old beds…"

"What in the world were you doing up there?"

"We were just exploring and we found two old beds, and can I have them? Where did they come from?"

"I haven't thought of that old stuff for years. Let me see if I can remember. Seems to me someone gave them to me ten or twelve years ago. What was that name? Wenzik, Westfall, started with a W. Wait."

He got up and reached into the bookshelf, pulled out a book, and leafed through it. He put it back, pulled out another.

"Here it is, Wentworth. I remember him now. His mother died, no money. He paid for the funeral with the two beds."

"That's so sad!"

"Well he insisted I should take the beds. It made him feel better. He felt bad enough over losing his mother."

"So, Grandfather, can I have the beds? I've never seen anything as beautiful as that four-poster bed."

"You can have them. I've no use for them. Are you sure your mother will want them?"

"I'm sure she will. Oh, thank you Grandfather."

"Now you and Mil will have to get them down by yourselves. I'm too busy to help. You'll have to clean them up and get them to your house. Don't make a mess, clean up after yourselves."

"We won't leave a mess. Thank you, thank you! I just love that four-poster bed and ..."

"Run along then, you've got lots of work to do."

One piece at a time Mil and I got all the posts of the two beds down the narrow stairs. We found old burlap sacks in the barn to clean the dust and dirt of years off the old beds. As each piece was uncovered, we found beautiful dark wood. Now, we had to get it all up to my house.

The side rails weren't too hard. We took two pieces at a time and stacked them in the garage. Mother was busy in the house, and my two sisters were at a party. Lu was fifteen and Marty, fourteen. They'd be home for dinner. I wanted to surprise them.

We managed to get the small bed home after two difficult trips. Then Mil had to go home. Her grandmother was so strict about meals that if Mil didn't get home in time, she didn't get anything to eat.

Now I was left with two huge pieces of the four-poster. After a great deal of struggling, I got one piece at a time across the street as far as Aunt Mary Warner's. I propped them on her fence and called her out to keep watch over my bed.

"Will you watch this bed while I run and get Mother to come and help me?"

"Where did you get that lovely bed? It must be one hundred years old."

"Grandfather gave it to me. Isn't it the most beautiful bed you've ever seen? Just like a bed for a princess!"

"I'll watch it for you. Run and get your mother."

Mother was surprised to see the old bed. She didn't remember ever having seen it. She supposed Grandfather just stored it in the shed as soon as he got it.

When we got home, I showed her the other bed, which was beautiful also, but not romantic like my four-poster.

"Did your Grandfather say you could have both beds?"

"Yes, he didn't want them. He said I could have them if I cleaned them up and didn't leave a mess. Mil and I cleaned everything and put all our cleaning stuff away. Isn't that the most romantic bed you've ever seen?!"

Mother looked so pleased. She thought for a minute, then she said, "I think I'll give the shorter bed to Marty and the four-poster to Lu."

I stood in stunned silence. To keep from crying I kept saying inside myself, "I don't care, I don't care, I don't care."

fragments

"Go upstairs now and get cleaned up," Mother said. "Dinner will be ready in a few minutes. The girls will be home and we'll surprise them. They'll be so excited!"

On each step as I stomped up the stairs, I kept saying "I don't care, I don't care, I don't care."

fragments

The Bus Trip

I was the last one to get on the bus. There were only two seats left. One was occupied by a very large lady who sat in the front seat, just behind the driver. A bulging carry-all and a large brown shopping bag lay on the seat beside her. She avoided looking at me. She looked so cross I knew she was discouraging me from sitting beside her.

The other seat was on the aisle beside a young boy. He was looking out the window. He looked safe enough. Maybe I'd be lucky and he wouldn't talk all the time. If there's anything I hate, it's to have to make idle chitchat with a stranger.

I threw my small bag on the overhead shelf and flopped down beside him. I hoped he wasn't going all the way to Boston so that I could move over to the window seat, and maybe luck out with the next passenger.

I looked at the other people on the bus and tried to figure out what they did and where they lived. Obviously, none of the passengers had any money, or they wouldn't be traveling on this old bus. They weren't students, either, because it was the wrong time of the year.

First, there is Peabody, our driver. I noticed his name when I got on the bus. How he came by the name of Peabody, I couldn't even guess. He was a small Italian; he had curly black hair and beautiful white teeth. He had a picture, pinned above the window, of a round little wife and two small children. He says he just loves driving the bus, and wouldn't want to do anything else. He whistles through his teeth as he drives, smiles at all the passengers, and helps them on and off the bus. He's a happy man!

150

fragments

There's a young woman with a baby she calls Charlie
sitting near the back of the bus. She keeps nervously
shushing him, but, so far, Charlie just smiles and murmurs
baby talk. I think she is probably going to meet her
husband and is nervous about her first trip with Charlie.

The woman in the front seat probably works for the
I.R.S. She looks like she'd enjoy intimidating anyone she
suspected was cheating the government out of a few dollars,
watching them cringe and turn into wimps right in front of
her eyes.

An elderly wisp of a woman sits across from me in the
aisle seat. She wears a little black hat beaten down on her
white hair. She carries a small worn black leather
pocketbook with a silver chain. She keeps opening it
nervously to check on her ticket.

I take a surreptitious glance at my seat mate. He looks
to be about eighteen, same as me. He has a thick mop of
dark hair, which he keeps pushing off his forehead. He has
nice hands—long fingers, short nails. He doesn't do much
hard work. I can just see him getting ready for the trip,
pressing his blue serge trousers, polishing his worn old
shoes, and borrowing a necktie from his dad. I wonder if
he's going to Boston.

He hasn't said a word. This is silly. "Are you going all
the way to Boston?" I ask.

"I live in Boston. I'm going home."

"Just been on a trip?"

"Been visiting my grandparents. I come once a year."

He continues looking out the window.

"What's your name?" As long as we're riding together
for two days and one night we may as well know who we
are."

"I'm Zack," he says.

"Not Zachary or Zacharias?"

"No, just Zack."

151

"Okay. Just Zack. I'm Wilma. I hate my name!"
"What's wrong with *Wilma*?"
"It makes me think of a fat old housewife."
"Who would you like to be?"
I consider that, and then say, "I think Catherine, Catherine with a *C.*"
Okay, Catherine with a C. That's what I'll call you."
An older man and woman sitting directly behind us are bickering and arguing. We listen unabashedly, intrigued with their conversation.
"I hope Agnes and Pearl are not too unhappy without us. You know what a baby Pearl is."
"Don't worry about her, Mildred. We've left them before. It isn't as if they were babies."
"Oh, you never worry about anything, Clyde. If you'd worry a little, we'd both be better off!"
"Worry gets you no place. Confound it, Mildred! Quit complaining."
Silence for a few minutes.
"I hope the girls get enough to eat," from Mildred.
I wonder what kind of parents these two are, and how old are these kids.
"Didn't Florence say she'd look in on them every evening?"
"Yes, she did. But what if she forgets?"
"Drop it, Mildred. I'm gonna enjoy this trip."
Now I suppose they're going to fight all the way to Boston!
Silence for awhile. The old bus rumbles over rough roads and potholes. Just Zack looks out the window. Fragile little lady opens her black pocketbook and checks her ticket. Surprise! It's still there.
"Let's have a sandwich at the next stop, Dear," Mildred says.
"Sounds good to me, Honey."

So, they aren't fighting, just married for a long time.

On the wide seat at the very back of the bus, a couple of cool dudes (at least they're trying to be cool) are holding big black cases. I hope they are guitars, and not guns. Actually, the boys don't look a bit dangerous. Kinda country. Later, I learn they are Tank and Tony. Tank is tall and thin, with long blond hair. He's wearing a brown sweater, brown trousers, sneakers, and no socks. Tony is all spiffed up in dark trousers and a very new plaid shirt, just off the rack at J.C. Penney's. They are going to Boston for their first gig in the big city. Probably been practicing in the garage since high school.

"We stop every three hours for twenty minutes," Just Zack informs me: "Time to stretch our legs and eat if we want to."

Our first stop is a little grocery store, a Mom-and-Pop store. Inside it's warm and cozy. They greet Peabody like an old friend. On the counter is a round glass rotisserie filled with hot dogs. They go around and roast and stay hot. Beside the hot dogs, there is a glass decanter filled with lemonade.

There's a small restroom for the men, and one for the women. *Grimface* gets off the bus first and makes a beeline to the restroom where she stays almost all of the twenty minutes. Other passengers stand outside and complain loudly. I learn quite early that the best way is to get off ahead of her. It isn't too difficult what with her considerable weight and her huge brown shopping bag, which she never lets out of her sight.

On one side of the store, there's a small area, about eight feet square, nice smooth floor, and a jukebox. Someone puts a nickel in, and music fills the room. I see Just Zack tapping his foot. I wonder if he can dance.

"Do you want to dance?" he asks.

I hesitate.

fragments

"I'm not asking you to the prom," he says, "just to dance."

I take his hand.

"You're good," I say in surprise. "Who taught you to dance?"

"My sister."

"She must be good."

"She teaches dancing at the Youth Center."

We dance for fifteen minutes. No time or money for food. Then we hear Peabody. He is honking the horn on the old bus, and yelling, "Last call, or we'll leave without you!"

The next stop, and all the stops afterwards, are much the same. Hot dogs and lemonade, restrooms, and a place to dance. We dance up a storm until Peabody yells. "You crazy kids, get on the bus. Next time I will leave without you." He's laughing. We know he won't do that.

Mildred wants to know if we'd like to see a picture of Pearl and Agnes.

"Sure," Zack says.

Mildred gets a picture out of her bag, hands it to Zack. I look over his shoulder. Then we both burst into laughter.

Mildred is indignant. "Well, I don't think it's all that funny," she says.

When we can stop laughing, I say, "We thought Pearl and Agnes were your children."

Mildred and Clyde think it's funny now and laugh with us. And there on the picture are two black and white cats.

Now, we have no trouble making conversation, and I learn that Just Zack is going to the Boston School of Music on a scholarship. He plays the piano, started when he was seven.

In the middle of the afternoon, ages since breakfast, Zack asks, "Would you like a sandwich? I have plenty. Grandma always packs too much."

154

fragments

"What kind?"

"Salami," he says, "with mustard and dill pickles."

Salami! I'm thinking. Nobody eats salami!

"No, thanks. I'm really not hungry."

"Okay," he says cheerfully.

He gets a bag off the overhead shelf, opens it carefully, and takes out a sandwich wrapped in wax paper. Thick, white slices of homemade bread, generous slices of salami, and wrapped separately, slices of dill pickle.

"Sure you don't want one?" he asks.

"No thanks."

He starts to eat. It smells wonderful. My stomach is doing flip-flops.

Zack grins. "You sure?"

"Well, maybe I'll try one."

He gets out another sandwich. I take a bite. I'm in heaven!

Now it's dark in the bus, except for the lights for Peabody. We rumble along over dirt roads and more potholes. Headlights pick up feral eyes along the road. Mildred and Clyde are asleep, leaning companionably on each other. There is an occasional whimper from Charlie, whispers from Tank and Tony. Then softly, sweetly, guitar music, *Moonlight and Roses.*

In all that quiet Zack whispers, "Are you sleepy?"

"Not really. It's kinda chilly. That keeps me awake."

It's harder and harder to keep my eyes open, the lull of the bus, the music---

I wake up slowly. I am leaning on Zack. His blue serge coat is around my shoulders. Out the window the sun is turning the sky to pink and pure gold.

"Oh! Zack, I'm sorry."

"Good morning to you, too," he says.

"I didn't mean to fall asleep. It was so peaceful."

"Anyway, it's time for our next stop."

155

fragments

So we dance our way through Ohio, Pennsylvania, New York, and Massachusetts. In the small grubby station in Boston, we say goodbye to the passengers who came all the way from Ohio. A special goodbye to Peabody.

Zack gives me a hug, and is off to join his family.

"Good luck with your music, Just Zack."

"Thanks for being my dance partner, Catherine with a *C*."

If anyone should ever ask me who was the first man I ever slept with, I would have to say it was Just Zack, in the bus, between Ohio and Boston.

fragments

A Night Out

Five o'clock and Bill and I are walking down Diamond Avenue with fifty cents between us, and we are extremely hungry. We are headed towards McCann's, our favorite place to eat. It is a huge market in downtown Pittsburgh where you can find everything in the world that is good to eat.

Tony greets us as we enter. He is wearing a white apron tied around his ample middle, and a white chef's hat covers all but a fringe of white hair. He is standing over a huge golden brown baked ham, holding an enormous knife.

"Is it a fine ham sandwich tonight, Kids? I'll make it extra special for you."

Tony can cut thin slices of succulent ham, stack it up between thick slices of crusty bread and slap on a bit of mustard before you can get your money out. They cost two dollars apiece. And the taste, well, you just have to try it. It makes you all warm and fuzzy to think about it.

"Afraid not tonight, Tony. Maybe next week."

He slices off two pieces and hands them to us on the big knife. "Just so you don't forget Tony," he says.

We go up the escalator, straight up to the third floor. Here we can get a doughnut and a cup of coffee for a nickel each. I get one doughnut; Bill gets two. We carry our empty cups and find a table. Mabel comes at once to fill our cups.

"How goes the art classes?" she asks.

"Fine, Mabel, just fine. I'll soon be rolling in wealth. Just a matter of time."

"I can wait," she says, saucily, "then I can say I knew you when."

She carries two huge pitchers, one with hot coffee, and the other with pure cream. Simultaneously, she pours both into my cup, frothy and creamy, then fills Bill's cup. If we can make the doughnuts last long enough, then Mabel will fill our cups up again. We chew them slowly, enjoying every bite. Tonight, we even get a third cup.

After we finish our coffee, we walk up Diamond Avenue to catch the streetcar at the corner of Fifth Avenue and Kaufmann's. Diamond is one of our favorite haunts. It is a whole different world. It runs parallel to Fifth Avenue, but where on Fifth, there are exclusive shops, department stores, and well-dressed people, Diamond is crowded and noisy and exciting.

The first shop we go into is small and cramped, and smells deliciously of garlic and peppers. Strings of purple onions and strings of figs hang from pegs on the wall. An array of lovely fresh vegetables fills one counter.

"Hi Luigi!"

"Hi Kids, how goes the art world?"

"We're surviving," Bill says.

"Are the doctors keeping you busy, Sugar?"

"Busy enough," I answer.

"You just let Luigi know if those doctors don't treat you right."

At Luigi's everyone is either fighting and screaming at each other or hugging and kissing. Whatever they do, it is done with a great deal of passion. They talk in Italian, and we understand about a fourth of what they say. But no matter, we love to listen. Tonight is a happy night. Luigi sings *O Sole Mio* in a fine baritone. Rippling with laughter, his wife Angie claps her hands and sways her round little body. Luigi, singing exuberantly, grabs me around the waist and dances me around past the purple onions, past the string of figs, and past the manicotti and the Italian sausage.

"Gotta go now, Luigi; dance with Angie. See you later."

Further on down the street, there's a place that sells thirty kinds of cheese. Joe cuts it off the huge round of cheese, which he keeps covered with glass. If you ask for a pound or even five pounds, he takes his big knife and cuts off the exact amount.

"Hi Joe, how are you doin'?"

Joe is short and fat, and his big white apron does nothing to enhance his appearance. He has a lovely smile, nice white teeth, and laughing eyes.

"Come on in, Kids. I have a new kind of cheese I want you to sample." He cuts off a couple of generous slices.

The cheese is delicious, but we aren't sure it is *actually* a new kind of cheese.

"Thanks, Joe! It's a wonderful cheese!"

Our next stop is Ruby and Pearl's. It can hardly be called a store, just a small nook off the street. They are mother and daughter, fat and jolly. They almost look alike in their flowered dresses and long black hair they've adorned with bright combs. They sell jars of homemade things—jams and jellies, relishes and pickles.

"Hi Ruby and Pearl! Selling lots of stuff?"

"Could be better, but we aren't complaining. What are you doing away from your classes?"

"We're celebrating. Bill sold a picture."

"Well, congratulations! We knew you could do it."

In the corner there is a huge wooden barrel full of pickles, five cents apiece. Bill gets the long fork and fishes out the biggest one he can find. We wander up the street sharing the dill pickle.

We stop at the burlesque theater, actually just a hole in the wall, and look at the glaring ads.

"Let's go in," I say.

"Oh, you wouldn't!"

"Yes, I would! I always wanted to see a burlesque show. What can it hurt? It's just a bunch of dancers."

"They aren't supposed to be very good dancers," Bill says.

"Did you ever go to a burlesque show?"

"No."

"Well, let's try it. If we don't like it, we can leave."

Tickets are ten cents. We look around to see if there is anyone we know, then quickly buy our tickets. The place is very dark and small. It smells like dirty clothes and urine and cheap perfume. There are, perhaps, twenty people scattered around, mostly men. They are slumped down in their seats, some with hats over their faces.

The music starts, a slow rumble, and a middle-aged woman with fat legs waddles onto the stage. She is heavily made up, has blonde frizzy hair piled high on her head. She doesn't look happy. I wonder if this is the only work she can get, and if she has children at home, and maybe a husband who is ill or doesn't have a job.

She does a few dance steps, no worse than the terrible music.

The men half-heartedly whistle. She takes off her feather boa. Another whistle. A few more dance steps and off comes her blouse. Now, the men whistle and stomp their feet, and the music gets louder.

I look at Bill, and we start to giggle. It's so funny! That fat woman up there taking off her clothes looking like a tired housewife, and those men stomping and whistling! Finally she is down to hot pink panties and bra, and she prances off. They want her back. They clap and whistle and stomp. We've had enough; we can't stop laughing. It's so funny, and yet, kind of sad, too.

We get to Kaufmann's just in time to catch our streetcar. We crowd on, show our passes. There are no seats. We

160

fragments

stand in the aisle, facing each other, hanging on to the straps.
The old streetcar rumbles and sways, and we are tumbled
happily together. We look at each other and laugh.
   What a great night out!

Snowstorm

It was early in the morning on a bright December day when my sister Lu and I decided we wanted to go shopping. My mother offered to go and take my little daughter, Marty, along. We left Alliance to go to Akron, a distance of about twenty-five miles.

I was quite confident as I drove off and waved goodbye to Dad.

"Enjoy the peace and quiet," I said, "We'll be back early."

We shopped all day and started home about five. It was starting to snow. The further we went, the heavier the snow fell. The wind picked up and the temperature quickly dropped. Soon the road was covered with inches of heavy white snow. It swirled around the car making the road barely visible. The windshield wipers couldn't push the heavy snow off. I tried to open a window and push it off, but the wind was fierce and I quickly knew that it wouldn't work. Mother and Lu never said a word, but we were all frightened. It was as if we were all holding our breath. I felt disoriented, never quite sure where the road was. I was moving at a snail's pace, gripping the steering wheel so hard my hands ached. Then slowly, irrevocably, we slid into a deep ditch.

I knew we were in trouble. For a few minutes I panicked. Collecting myself, I remembered that you were supposed to stay in your car and wait for help, but we had less than half a tank of gas which probably wouldn't keep us warm all night. We had no extra blankets and no food. I didn't think my mother and Marty could make it until help came.

We decided to abandon the car and seek shelter. I had misgivings. I remembered hearing about a woman who went out to her mailbox in a blizzard, became disoriented, and froze to death. But staying in the car was also unthinkable.

In the distance I could see, flickering through the snow, one of those gas lights that burn all the time on farms. If I could keep my eyes on that light, I knew it would lead us to a farmhouse or a barn and shelter.

Lu and I were wearing heavy coats, gloves, and scarves. Mother had a heavy coat and a silly hat. I wrapped my scarf around Mother's head, half covering her face to protect it from the biting wind. I carried Marty wrapped securely in a small baby blanket. We set out together.

The snow was now almost two feet deep on this back road. We knew we couldn't risk getting separated. I led the way with the baby. Mother followed hanging onto my coat; Lu held onto Mother's coat. I knew I was responsible for these three people who meant more to me than the whole world. I prayed that I would find shelter.

In the dim distance I could see the light. "I see it!" I yelled. "Hang on; we're going to be alright!"

After what seemed like hours we stumbled onto the porch of a big house. Mrs. Emma Miller heard us yelling, opened her door and we literally fell in, weeping thankful tears and feeling the wonderful warmth of that old house. Luckily, the telephone was still in operation so we called Dad to tell him we were safe. We knew, however, that it might be days before we could get our car out and start home.

Mother was never one to sit idly by. "Do you have any mending or sewing I could do?" she asked. "We can't just sit here and impose on you."

"I bought several pieces of material for dresses," Emma said. "Maybe you could help me with one of them."

We got organized. Mother and Lu started on the dresses. Mother sewed on the machine; Lu did the hand work. I cooked the meals with plenty of food from the freezer.

Emma was in seventh heaven taking care of Marty, a bouncy two-year-old with blue eyes, red curls, and a smile to melt your heart.

The storm subsided on the fourth day and Emma's son, Tony, got through to us with his tractor. He rescued our car. It was not damaged and we were able to start home. We had walked half a mile in that raging storm! Surely an angel had been watching over us!

We had all had a frightening, but wonderful adventure. Emma had six new dresses, and we had a new friend.

fragments

My Brothers and Sisters

When I remember that day so many years ago, it's to bring back a time of innocence, a time rich, sweet, and warm. Now as I write this I think of the words of William Butler Yeats.

> *Come away! 0, human child!*
> *To the woods and waters wild.*
> *With a fairy hand in hand,*
> *For the world's more full of weeping than*
> *You can understand.*

A friend came into my father's store and told him that there was a bumper crop of butternuts that year. There was a tree deep in the woods on his farm, and if he wanted to bring the children, they could have all the butternuts they could pick up.

So on a bright October day we set out. The air was crisp and the pale winter sun made shafts of light through the dark branches.

My father had brought a robe for Mother to sit on. It was one of those double robes that we used in cars before they had heaters. It looked like fur, black on one side, brown on the other. He spread it on the ground near the butternut tree, and my beautiful little mother with one year old Ginny watched the children gather butternuts. I remember Mother was wearing a long tweed coat, green I think, and baby Ginny was in a red coat and hood trimmed in white fur. She was laughing and happy that day.

My father didn't pick up butternuts. He was the overseer. He was tall, broad-shouldered, self- assured. I never heard my father laugh out loud, but I know he was happy in his own quiet way. He was proud of his hardware store and of all of us (although he never told us he was). He was, however, known to brag that he had seven kids and they had all graduated from college.

My oldest sister, Lu, was quietly and carefully filling her basket with nuts. My sister Marty was keeping us all laughing with her smart remarks; Milt and Jimmy were chasing each other, tumbling around like a couple of puppies, incidentally, gathering nuts. My beautiful little three-year-old brother Charlie was picking up nuts, one or two at a time, placing them in his wicker basket and taking them to Mother, then running on little boy legs for another trip.

There we were so many years ago, the whole family with no shadows over us. The world was ours.

I'll tell you about Lu first. Everyone thought she was beautiful with her dreamy eyes and her soft dark hair. I never thought she was beautiful at the time. She was just my oldest sister. She was always delicate and fragile. By the time she was fourteen, she was playing the violin at social gatherings. People used to say she looked and played like an angel. When she was fifteen, she had something wrong with her leg and was in a cast for almost a year. My father built an arbor in the back yard, covered it with pale pink climbing roses. On summer days she spent hours there with her books and music. I don't know how much she read because half the boys in the neighborhood came to see the rose arbor. At least that's what they told my father.

She graduated from college Phi Beta Kappa, and May Queen. She married a doctor. They had two bright healthy children, a beautiful house, and the doctor had a lucrative practice. At the time she told me she had it all.

Then her husband was drafted. He spent the next four years in a MASH unit. Lu waited out the lonely years. I spent a great deal of time with her back then. Everything during those war years was so crazy. We spent hours with an ouija board, asking it over and over if our husbands were safe, and when they'd be coming home. We didn't really believe in ouija boards but it gave us something to do. Sometimes in the middle of the night we'd get up and decide to bake a chocolate cake or an apple pie, and then stay up all night eating. Oh, things were all mixed up during those war years! Then finally her husband came home. He was different. He would sit and gaze into space, not talking. He resumed his practice. He was impatient with people who complained of stomach ache, a cut finger, a ticklish throat. Human life didn't seem important to him anymore. Within a year he went down into his basement and killed himself.

Marty was entirely different, very outgoing, always laughing and making others laugh. She didn't care much about grades. She was always a little overweight, wore outrageous clothes, and had beautiful light curly hair. She was musical, too. She played the organ and sang funny songs to the kids in the neighborhood who came to listen and sing along with her.

She was a trained nurse, so when the war needed nurses, she enlisted and was commissioned as a lieutenant. She was placed in a hospital ward with young boys. All of them had been seriously wounded, some with both legs gone, some with no arms, some blind. As she made her rounds giving comfort and medicine that did little to ease their pain, they begged her to just let them die. After years of this, she broke down and was given a medical discharge.

Years later, I visited Marty in a veterans' home. No one was permitted to take in any kind of food. She was on a strict diet because she had gained quite a bit of weight.

"Could you bring me a chocolate milkshake?" she asked me first thing when I got there. She sounded so sick!

"I can't; you aren't allowed milkshakes."

"I've been thinking about a chocolate milkshake for days. Please bring me one."

"I couldn't get it in here. They check everything I'm carrying."

"Please, please, just a little one. Couldn't you put it in your pocketbook?"

"I could never get it in. Try and think about something else."

"You could put some in a jar with a lid and put it in your pocketbook. They'd never see it. Please. I do want a milkshake."

But I couldn't.

As I left she looked at me pleadingly. "Please," she said.

Two days later, she died. All she wanted was a milkshake, a small, chocolate milkshake!

Milt was rather small and had very bad eyesight. As he was gathering butternuts, I'm sure he was scheming ways he could sell them and make money. He used to pull a small red wagon filled with vegetables from my grandfather's farm, and sell the produce to the neighbors.

He had a vocabulary that was amazing. He read the dictionary every day to learn new words. He used the words over and over until they were his own. He loved to argue and debate. No matter what the subject, he'd take the opposite side and argue. It could be annoying until you realized that he just loved to argue. He was a CPA, always had an excellent job.

When the war started, he tried to enlist but was turned down because of his eyes. I think this had a profound effect on the rest of his life. And although he worked in a munitions factory all during the war years, he started to drink. When the war ended he had no trouble getting a job. He was super-smart. He'd get a good high-paying job, keep it maybe six months or a year, go on a binge, get fired, get another good job and keep it until the next binge. He tried really hard to stop drinking.

He loved good books and especially poetry. Sometimes when he was home he'd call me into his room and we'd sit on the bed and read poetry.

In the middle of the night I got a call from him. In a scarcely coherent voice he said, "Help me, Willie. I can't hang on!"

I got there too late.

Jim was to lead a charmed life. He, too, was a CPA and super-smart. Oh, I guess they were all super-smart! He had dreams of traveling to faraway places even when he was a small boy. So after two years as an officer in the Navy he came home to Bette, the love of his life. Even though he had shrapnel in both legs he suffered no other damage.

He had jobs as comptroller in Arabia, Bermuda, Jamaica, Cuba, and Virginia. Jim was quite handsome, a little arrogant and sometimes ruthless, but, unbelievably kind and fair. When Jim and Bette lived in Cuba, Jim was comptroller for Portland Cement. Castro confiscated all his money, car, most of his household goods and ordered him out of Cuba. Jim swore if he ever met Castro face to face he'd kill him.

Later in Jamaica with Reynolds Aluminum, the company held a gala celebration to honor Castro who was coming for a visit. Jim was invited and, as he was being introduced to Castro, Bette stepped back to take Jim's picture. She giggled as Jim shook hands with Castro.

Charlie, my youngest brother, unlike the other boys who had dark hair and eyes, was blond and blue-eyed. He was six feet tall, the most lovable and gentle and just so good and wholesome that everyone loved him. He played football in college but didn't have much of a social life because he

worked very hard to earn his way through college.
He worked in an ice cream parlor. Sometimes it was
after midnight when he got home. At the end of the day,
ice cream containers that were nearly empty were taken out
and filled up ready for the next day. Charlie brought the
leftover ice cream home and he and Mother and Dad would
enjoy it. I think Charlie was closer to my parents, especially
Mother, than any of the rest of us.

He was making plans to go to medical school, but the
day he graduated from college, he got his letter from Uncle
Sam. After officer's training he spent four years in the
infantry. At 23 he was a captain. He came home with a
purple heart and a bronze star. He had rescued four men
from a burning tank.

He fell in love and married Sara. They had a few happy
years together. Then Charlie suffered a stroke and Sara left
him.

For the next fifteen years I took care of Charlie. He
lived in the veterans' home near me. He spent every holiday
and most weekends with me and my family. We all loved
Charlie. He was bright and articulate, kept up with the news,
helped me refinish furniture, husked the corn in summer,
and made the stuffing for the chicken or turkey. He loved
the lake and could sit for hours counting the boats and
enjoying the wildlife. But the few years after the stroke
were a complete blank. So for the next fifteen years he
waited for Sara to come for him.

One night when we were taking him home, as we drove
down Rye Beach Road, there was a spectacular sunset. We
pulled over and Charlie, who has going back to one small
room at a veterans' home, Charlie said, "By golly, it makes a
fellow glad to be alive!" That was Charlie!

I was at the veterans' home just before he died. I do not
look like Sara although we were about the same size and
both had dark hair. As I entered the room on that last day

he suddenly sat up in bed, smiled with such joy on his ravaged face and said, "Oh, Sara you've come for me!"

Ginny and I lived far from each other. I saw her when she came home on special days but there were always about twenty others there. I talked to her on the phone at least twice a month, but not about anything important. She said I always made her laugh.

I went to her funeral a few years ago. The service was in a very small country church in Rhode Island. Everyone wanted to talk with me because they thought I looked so much like Ginny. From those friends who loved her I found out more about her than I ever knew.
I learned that she played the guitar and sang and had made a record. She played the piano for church. She taught first grade in a private school. She went to the prison one day a week and taught reading to the inmates. She took cookies once a week to the people in a retirement home. She wrote short pieces for the local paper.

My little sister!

My brothers and sisters were strong and for the most part they coped rather well. They married, had children and grandchildren. Every Thanksgiving and 4th of July, they came to my parent's home from all over the country where cousins, uncles, and aunts would spend two wonderful days feasting and laughing and simply enjoying each other.

I'm sure there were days full of the sheer joy of just being alive, magic moments for all of us and delight in everyday things. And always, we had books and music.

Tragedy and joy. Life!

And we loved each other.

About the author:

Wilma Daugherty was born in East Palestine, Ohio. She was one of seven children growing up in a household surrounded by books and music. After graduating from high school in Alliance, Ohio, she attended Grove City College in western Pennsylvania. There, she met her husband Bill. They were married for fifty years.

A graduate of Bowling Green State University, she has two children, two grandchildren, and five great-grandchildren. Wilma has been a gifted storyteller her whole life, and a writer for nearly as long.

Printed in the United States
83138LV00002B/61-108/A